Social Education for Peace

Other Palgrave Pivot titles

Dilip K. Das: **An Enquiry into the Asian Growth Model**

Jan Pakulski and Bruce Tranter: **The Decline of Political Leadership in Australia? Changing Recruitment and Careers of Federal Politicians**

Christopher W. Hughes: **Japan's Foreign and Security Policy under the 'Abe Doctrine': New Dynamism or New Dead End?**

Eleanor Sandry: **Robots and Communication**

Hyunjung Lee: **Performing the Nation in Global Korea: Transnational Theatre**

Creso M. Sá and Andrew J. Kretz: **The Entrepreneurship Movement and the University**

Emma Bell: **Soft Power and Freedom under the Coalition: State-Corporate Power and the Threat to Democracy**

Ben Ross Schneider: **Designing Industrial Policy in Latin America: Business-State Relations and the New Developmentalism**

Tamer Thabet: **Video Game Narrative and Criticism: Playing the Story**

Raphael Sassower: **Compromising the Ideals of Science**

David A. Savage and Benno Torgler: **The Times They Are A Changin': The Effect of Institutional Change on Cooperative Behaviour at 26,000 ft over Sixty Years**

Mike Finn (editor): **The Gove Legacy: Education in Britain after the Coalition**

Clive D. Field: **Britain's Last Religious Revival? Quantifying Belonging, Behaving, and Believing in the Long 1950s**

Richard Rose and Caryn Peiffer: **Paying Bribes for Public Services: A Global Guide to Grass-Roots Corruption**

Altug Yalcintas: **Creativity and Humour in Occupy Movements: Intellectual Disobedience in Turkey and Beyond**

Joanna Black, Juan Carlos Castro, and Ching-Chiu Lin: **Youth Practices in Digital Arts and New Media: Learning in Formal and Informal Settings**

Wouter Peeters, Andries De Smet, Lisa Diependaele and Sigrid Sterckx: **Climate Change and Individual Responsibility: Agency, Moral Disengagement and the Motivational Gap**

Mark Stelzner: **Economic Inequality and Policy Control in the United States**

Michelle Bayefsky and Bruce Jennings: **Regulating Preimplantation Genetic Diagnosis in the United States**

Eileen Piggot-Irvine: **Goal Pursuit in Education Using Focused Action Research**

Serenella Massidda: **Audiovisual Translation in the Digital Age: The Italian Fansubbing Phenomenon**

John Board, Alfonso Dufour, Yusuf Hartavi, Charles Sutcliffe and Stephen Wells: **Risk and Trading on London's Alternative Investment Market: The Stock Market for Smaller and Growing Companies**

Franklin G. Mixon, Jr: **Public Choice Economics and the Salem Witchcraft Hysteria**

Elisa Menicucci: **Fair Value Accounting: Key Issues Arising from the Financial Crisis**

Nicoletta Pireddu: **The Works of Claudio Magris: Temporary Homes, Mobile Identities, European Borders** palgrave▸pivot

Social Education for Peace: Foundations, Teaching, and Curriculum for Visionary Learning

Candice C. Carter
Associate Dean, College of Education and Counseling Psychology, Saint Martin's University, US

palgrave
macmillan

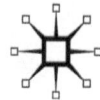

SOCIAL EDUCATION FOR PEACE
Copyright © Candice C. Carter, 2015.

All rights reserved.

First published in 2015 by
PALGRAVE MACMILLAN®
in the United States—a division of St. Martin's Press LLC,
175 Fifth Avenue, New York, NY 10010.

Where this book is distributed in the UK, Europe and the rest of the world, this is by Palgrave Macmillan, a division of Macmillan Publishers Limited, registered in England, company number 785998, of Houndmills, Basingstoke, Hampshire RG21 6XS.

Palgrave Macmillan is the global academic imprint of the above companies and has companies and representatives throughout the world.

Palgrave® and Macmillan® are registered trademarks in the United States, the United Kingdom, Europe and other countries.

ISBN: 978-1-137-53406-4 EPUB
ISBN: 978-1-137-53405-7 PDF
ISBN: 978-1-137-54273-1 Hardback

Library of Congress Cataloging-in-Publication Data is available from the Library of Congress.

A catalogue record of the book is available from the British Library.

First edition: 2015

www.palgrave.com/pivot

DOI: 10.1057/9781137534057

This work is dedicated to educators who stimulate students to search for, study, and shape peace.

Contents

List of Illustrations	vii
Acknowledgments	ix
Introduction	1
1 Foundations of Social Education for Peace	5
2 Peace-Focused Policy for Social Education	29
3 Responsive Curriculum and Instruction	47
4 Transdisciplinary and Powerful Learning	72
5 Mindful and Engaged Citizenship	92
Appendix: Standards for Peace Education	120
References	130
Name Index	162
Subject Index	170

List of Illustrations

Figures

5.1	Ripples from our actions	95
5.2	Components of disposition development	97
5.3	Perspective triangulation	100
5.4	Envisioning peace	102

Tables

1.1	Lakota principles	8
1.2	Purposes and principles of Soka Gakkai's Charter	15
1.3	Visioning as curriculum	18
1.4	Domains of conflict transformation	21
1.5	Capability goals	22
1.6	Case example: dramatic performances that demonstrate peace	23
1.7	Lesson plan: playwriting about peace	24
2.1	Compassionate communication lesson with the learning cycle	34
2.2	Code-switching activity with compassionate communication	35
2.3	Case example: state standards	38
2.4	Educational organizations in the US providing recommendations	39
2.5	Instructional planning with related standards: lesson plan	42

3.1	Modes of curriculum modification for diversity knowledge and response	51
3.2	Hidden curriculum	58
3.3	Transformation of knowledge	61
3.4	Case example: the singing strike and the rebel students singing	63
3.5	Identification and communication with others connected in conflict: lesson plan	67
4.1	Traditional disciplines of social education	75
4.2	Emergent disciplines of social education	75
4.3	Concept-based learning within and across subject areas	76
4.4	Futures contents in the themes of social education	86
4.5	Case example: kids in action	87
4.6	Interdependent workers: lesson plan	88
5.1	Case example: peace seeds newsletter	111
5.2	Children's rights instruction: lesson plan	116

Acknowledgments

Development of this book, during a time of much transition in my life, occurred with the crucial assistance of Ian Harris, Amanda Laukitis, and Aline Stomfay-Stitz. This book is a tribute to my parents whose lives oriented me toward social inquiry and action. I greatly appreciate the support and understanding of my husband and children during the production of this book.

palgrave▸pivot

www.palgrave.com/pivot

Introduction

Carter, Candice C. *Social Education for Peace: Foundations, Teaching, and Curriculum for Visionary Learning.* New York: Palgrave Macmillan, 2015. DOI: 10.1057/9781137534057.0004.

Social education builds learners' understanding of and civic participation in their society. The National Council for the Social Studies (2008) in the USA advocates powerful and authentic social studies. For that purpose, it includes issues as content in the social studies. Learning about current as well as past conflicts humans have faced involves development of students' knowledge, skills, and dispositions (KSD) that support democratic responses to societal challenges. The multiple disciplines included in social education provide a spectrum of possibilities for problem solving. Students can learn about how people in many fields have developed strategies for addressing challenges. Learners need to know how people were ethical by interacting well with others in response to conflict.

A hope for humanity is problem solving without violence. That achievement involves work for the protection of not only environments, but also relationships in them. Non-harmful relations optimize possibilities for life in the condition of well-being. Harm's multiplying effects reveal the interdependence of lives. Hence, peace is a relevant topic for all people, regardless of their current life circumstances. A vision of humanity's peaceful coexistence, with each other and other life forms, is crucial in achievement of that goal. As examinations of peace accomplishments reveal, envisioning a better situation precedes the actual manifestation of that pictured circumstance. In education, and many other facets of life, expectations determine student success. Teachers can plan for and expect student development of the KSD that support non-harmful conflict management and the creation of problem solutions. People encounter problems in multiple situations where they can use the KSD's of non-harm in their pursuit of solutions.

Peace is a situational concept that represents what people in a particular time and place encounter, and then feel and do as a response. It typically involves recognition of unmet needs that impede well-being. Humans bring about and maintain peace by use of every discipline that social education includes: psychology, sociology, anthropology, geography, economics, political science, history and humanities. Accordingly, the concept of peace has a place in each of these strands.

With a focus on well-being, peace education occurs through the experience of learning about the world, its condition, and its inhabitants. It has a wide-angle lens for examining locations from the inner mind to the galaxy. The condition of each of those places and how humans use them are topics of peace-oriented social education. Identity, for instance, has been a focus topic in education because it associates with instructional outcomes and well-being. There is a recommendation for reinstating the materiality of things and practices by focusing on the construction of the world, instead of analyzing its composition (Zemblas & Bekerman, 2013). In other words, focusing on identity as the source of conflict overlooks the situation that caused a conflict for one or more identities. Ethnicity, for example, is not the focus in a situation that evidences unequal allocation of resources. Rights and inequity are the foci of that conflict. This is not to say that identity is unimportant. Reframing from identity as an unchanging and context-free construct enables recognition of its composition at a particular time and place. Being a citizen and an activist varies in different periods and locations of the world. There are contextual perceptions of a person pursuing peace through social, economic, political, or environmental justice. Analysis from each viewpoint clarifies needs in each of them. With an environmental perspective, a citizen can see the cost of a production practice that an economic perspective overlooks. While the condition of stability may mean peace to one, the accomplishment of change is the desire of another. Clarification of their needs and visions of harm-free production precede steps toward that development.

One strand of social education is the construal of peace throughout human history and what people believed characterized that condition. How one might experience peace in the future as well as in the present is another strand. Students need opportunities to learn about how humans and other life forms have worked through conflict. They can then think about how people will solve problems in the future without further harm. This book supports such learning. It offers examples of peace education as well as suggestions for its facilitation. The information includes ways in which school and community members can use informal as well as formal learning situations within and beyond schools for visionary social education. Those learning opportunities can build vital hope and stimulate creativity for constructing and maintaining peace.

An orientation to the chapters illuminates notions of peace and opportunities for its inclusion in social education. Chapter 1 describes how people in different regions and time periods have thought about peace. It then presents contents of modern peace education, including envisioning and conflict management. Chapter 2 examines policies that affect peace-oriented social education. In addition to analyzing effects of policies, it presents theoretical foundations of peace education and voluntary standards for that pedagogy. Chapter 3 elaborates domains of informal as well as formal education. It describes the affective, cognitive, and practical realms of learning in social education. Chapter 4 brings awareness of different forms of knowledge that humans can use in the pursuit of peace. Transdisciplinary and powerful learning incorporates emergent as well as traditional ways of thinking and connecting in social education. Chapter 5 designates the types of awareness for comprehensive citizenship. It discusses social, environmental, ethical, geographic, economic, and political citizenship. All of the chapters address how people construe peace and strategies for its development. Students need awareness that humans continually desire and work for peace. Learners deserve opportunities in social education for participation in that pursuit.

Reference

Zembylas, M., & Bekerman, Z. (2013). Peace education in the present: Dismantling and reconstructing some fundamental theoretical premises. *Journal of Peace Education*, 10(2), 197–214.

1
Foundations of Social Education for Peace

Abstract: *Notions of peace and how people accomplish it have existed worldwide, for millennia. The precursor to the accomplishments was envisioning peace. While principles of spiritual and indigenous traditions provided signposts for paths to peace, harmful responses to conflict also stimulated peace efforts. Eastern philosophies and Western ideologies offer the connected world a solid foundation for building peace in all regions. Students can learn global peace concepts and develop visioning skills in each of the subject areas. This chapter identifies other capability goals in peace education as well as domains of conflict transformation and provides a case example of students' peace dramas.*

Carter, Candice C. *Social Education for Peace: Foundations, Teaching, and Curriculum for Visionary Learning.* New York: Palgrave Macmillan, 2015.
DOI: 10.1057/9781137534057.0005.

Theoretical foundations

Forming the foundation of social education for peace are notions that spanned millennia as well as recent ones in the past two centuries. There are multiple ideas about how people might live together in a condition of peace. Modern peace education was constructed with such conceptions and research that analyzed their implementation. Teachers have incorporated as curriculum the conflicts in their society and world. Their motivation for active response to societal and students' needs is a crucial component of visionary education as well as peace-oriented citizenship. Proactive people who address conflict apply theories that are foundations of social education and peace development (Carter & Kumar, 2010; Diamond, 2000; Nagler, 2004). The prosocial stance of peace educators and peacemakers has foundational ideas about how a society could improve its situation, especially through the avoidance of violence. The term *prosocial* refers to an orientation that may be evident in dispositions or skills known for supporting improvement of society. The motivation for prosocial modeling comes from a desire for improvement of circumstances where harmful responses to conflict exist. Envisioning other types of responses is the crucial work of educators and their students on the ideological paths that peacemakers have made.

Throughout the world, people have envisioned peace and then taken action with the use and augmentation of existing ideas. People who pursued peace have also advanced new ideas. Many of their accomplishments, which peace history documents, occurred after they pictured better situations than the ones they observed or knew about (Curti, 1985). Ian Harris (2008) explains how wars in Europe and then a world war stimulated the formation of peace societies whose members called for education to prevent war. Organizations that held visions of life without violence, like the Women's International League for Peace and Freedom, are peace societies. While a disposition toward social responsibility or stewardship was evident in the minds of many proactive people during the past century, professors, teachers, and mentors motivated others. Informing about notions of and goals for societal and personal improvement have been important lessons that teachers, as well as community and family elders, sages, and spiritual leaders, provided. Conceptions of a good society have been germane while ideas about how to bring about "the good" have varied. These variations exist as diverse ideas and means for maintaining a good society (Bellah et al., 1991; Dajani, 2006). They are worthwhile considerations for students acquiring visionary social education in a multicultural world (Mills, 1997).

Principles across spiritual traditions

Principles are the ethical standards in a society that have held people socially, and sometimes legally, accountable. They serve as guideposts of right action for the well-being of the society or the culture that maintains the principles as ideological and behavioral codes, if not membership criteria. Principles traditionally provided by scriptures promote envisioning. For example, Proverbs 29:18 of the Bible states, "Where there is not vision, people perish..." (Bible Study Tools, August 4, 2013, para. 1). Principled living that sustains a society occurs through picturing how that way of life can occur. Consequently, each society has had a foundation of clarified principles that enabled peaceful interaction between its members. The book *Spirituality, Religion, and Peace Education* (Brantmeier, Lin, & Miller, 2010) provides in-depth descriptions of how the principles served as the foundation of learning and guidelines for peace in many world regions.

It is important to acquire knowledge about principles that support unity across cultures and regions. The principles of a culture offer visions of and standards for a good life. For example, many cultures have edicts to sustain and preserve human life. A comparison of principles in various religions reveals the commonality of people in different cultures. People desire a life in the condition of peace. When viewing differences of surface culture as interesting rather than objectionable, comprehension of deep commonalities across cultures supports a disposition of acceptance. Modeling by adults of acceptance when they encounter cultural differences facilitates this disposition development by youth who see that behavior. In other words, cultivation of acceptance happens during observation of that enacted disposition as well as in demonstrations of curiosity about cultural differences (Pate, 1997). The principle of unity within a culture is evident worldwide. There is unity in diversity across cultures as well as within one society. Diversity of thoughts and skills has been crucial for survival, especially in the face of conflict. Experts in conflict resolution and transformation have identified how helpful it is to have different perspectives of a problem included in the work for its solution (Lederach, 2003). A component of indigenous peace as well as current conflict work by specialists in problem solving is the ideology of unity. The notion of unity orients humans toward cooperation and interdependence as a community of life forms.

Indigenous concepts

Indigenous concepts of peace have existed throughout the world. Enduring concepts of peace in the daily living of indigenous people influence their avoidance of and solutions for problems (Odora Hoppers, 2002; Ramose, 1996). For example, the African concept of *e Munthu* (Malawian language) that translates as "humanness" expresses a notion of fraternity in a community. To be fully human, one must interact well with others, thereby demonstrating ethical responsibility (Sharra, 2006).

From the Indigenous Peoples of North America, we have similar viewpoints, illustrated by examples in Table 1.1 from the Lakota People (Four Arrows, 2010, p. 137).

The laws known as the Great Peace, which the Iroquois Confederacy has maintained for many centuries, articulate the responsibilities of individuals and groups within and across communities to maintain ethical interactions. Included in the laws of the Iroquois are notions of conflict management and dispute resolution with a future orientation. For example, Law 26 calls on political leaders to serve as mentors and spiritual guides with use of the following statement.

> Hearken, that peace may continue unto future days!
> Always listen to the words of the Great Creator, for he has spoken.
> United people, let not evil find lodging in your minds.
> For the Great Creator has spoken and the cause of Peace shall not become old.
> (Murphy & National Public Telecomputing Network, 2012)

TABLE 1.1 *Lakota principles*

Wowayuonihan	To have respect and give significance to all creations
Wowahwala	Humility—this relates to genuine belief that no one is above another; no superior to the rest of creation. When one embraces this, it is difficult to practice enmity or prejudice to rationalize violence
Wolokokiciapi	Peacefulness within oneself and with all others—this recognizes that the natural state of all life emphasizes peacefulness, but that we must constantly work to develop the virtues to assure that we cannot be misled from the peaceful path

Incorporated into the Aboriginal worldview, with the notion of the "Dreaming" that preceded all creation, is vision. As envisioned in the Dream, peace results from compliance with "the law" that embodies the rules for living well in the created world (Tonkinson, 2004). Modes of living to manifest the Dream vary across regions and cultures. Diversity in pursuit of peaceful lives is normal and interesting to learn about in oral and written accounts (Mathis, 2001).

Literature about the pursuit of peace in traditional societies reveals people have had similar notions and processes of peacemaking, although there are differences in particular norms. One common strand has been methods for peaceful communication and exchange across cultures. With differences in values and norms that distinguish cultures, careful social interaction can maintain optimal relations between groups. Balance and mutuality necessitate good relations across as well as within groups (MacGinty, 2008).

Strands of indigenous peacemaking that have recently been adapted into modern society are restoration of relations through compensation for losses, honoring the harmed, and other processes (Carter, 2010b). For example, modern peace initiatives incorporated from indigenous practices include Circles for communication about harm and restoration of well-being. A Circle is a process in which people meet for communication together. Participation in a Circle by all affected people enables sharing of perspectives while it can convey interest in addressing the needs that the harmful act evidenced, in addition to the outcomes of the harm. Schools as well as other community organizations now use Circles for problem solving with a future orientation (Pranis, 2005). With an orientation toward restoration of peace, schools have been unknowingly following in the footsteps of indigenous peoples by taking steps to restore damaged relationships and develop new ones that improve social interactions in the learning environment (Amstutz & Mullet, 2005; Cavanagh, 2009). Faith groups around the world adapted restorative practices of First Nations, long before education became secularized. In *The Spiritual Roots of Restorative Justice* (Hadley, 2001), the contributors of each chapter identify how restoration has been occurring in many spiritual as well as religious traditions. The book identifies these enduring practices as expressions of human hope that have been evident in a multitude of faiths and regions. Awareness of the worldwide notions of peace and paths to it that people have taken throughout human history, across religious and spiritual traditions, builds understanding of human commonality in the desire for peace. To counteract cultural polarities that are evident in discourse about conflicts between groups, educators emphasize how people in each group have used their own culture's notions of peace in response to violent conflict.

Eastern philosophies

In the Eastern Hemisphere, visions of peace became enduring philosophical and spiritual traditions that Westerners have adopted. For example, a notion that educators as well as many others have fused in their responses to conflict, if not their daily practices, is the Tao (the Way). The Way involves simple and harmonious living with people and all of nature. In the *Tao of Teaching* (1998), Greta Nagel shares through stories about teaching in the USA how the Tao influenced personal as well as professional actions, and non-actions, that have a peace orientation. For example, she applies the goal of balance that *yin* and *yang* represent. Methods to pursue the Way are balance of gender representation in the curriculum and classroom interaction as well as teacher and student talk time. Additionally, balancing one's work and relaxation time enhances one's ability to benefit others, due to increased personal contentment. Another facet of Taoism is facilitation of harmony. The ideal is human balance with nature as well as with other people, especially in the fulfillment of life-sustaining needs. The modern ecological movement resonates with reverence for nature in pursuit of the Tao. Other philosophical traditions also express the notion of balance and harmony.

Buddhism promotes the idea of the Middle Way, which is a path of moderation that avoids extremes, such as destructive behaviors with the self and others (Yeh, 2006). Nirvana, which translates to enlightenment, derives from the elimination of dualities that obscure progress on the path to peace. Justification of destruction is an outcome of a dualistic viewpoint that rationalizes harm. Principles of Jainism and Buddhism recognize harm of anything as harm to everything. The Sanskrit term *ahimsa*, which is a life principle for Jains and Buddhists, refers to doing no harm, or nonviolence. In lessons about life choices of Mohandas Gandhi and the founder of Buddhism, Siddhartha Gautama, teachers can provide examples of living in accordance with these notions. For example, the organization Soka Gakkai International applies the principles of Buddhism in current educational and cultural activities. Students learn how Gautama, known as Buddha, eschewed the material well-being he inherited. This facilitated his enlightenment and a way of life that benefited others who were suffering, especially from poverty. In their study of Gandhi, known as the Mahatma ("Great Soul" in Sanskrit), Martin Luther King Jr., who adopted the Mahatma's strategies, and Nelson Mandela, who applied them in South Africa, students learn how nonviolent action brought about needed change where social injustice existed. The notion of *satyagraha*, or insistence for truth, was a foundational principle of visionary political actions in response to injustice. With truth (*satya*) and firmness (*agraha*), major efforts to eliminate oppression continue to be successful in bringing about envisioned changes throughout the world. Instead of passive resistance that Westerners, such as the female suffragettes, used to bring about political changes, those who embraced *satyagraha* engaged in activities that prompted oppositional responses. The attention such situations garnered highlighted the need for ending oppression. Grounded in Buddhist notions of truth, specifically the Four Noble Truths, was the steadfast promotion of democracy that Aung San Suu Kyi maintained in Myanmar (formerly Burma), while she endured physical attacks and years of imprisonment. *Dukkha Niroda Gamini Patipada*, the fourth truth, describes the pathway to freedom from suffering. Recognized through the many awards bestowed on her, including the Nobel Peace Prize, are the efforts of Suu Kyi to enact her vision with others of democracy in Myanmar. Her concern for others, which resulted in her conviction for protecting an American trespasser at her property during her house arrest, also illustrates tenets of another Eastern philosophy. Mohism resulted from the notions of Mozi in China. His notions of universal love and no fatalism have been evident in the peace pursuits of Westerners as well as Easterners. Instead of accepting suffering as destiny, Mozi proposed that well-being comes from decisions people make. They can choose to eliminate harm and pursue peace. A vision of a good life was one without ostentation as well as poverty. Contemplation and communication support identification of what materials are truly necessary for life. Thinkers in the West who contemplated and articulated peace processes have fortified peace education.

Western ideologies

Relatively recent in the West are notions that have supported visions of peace through education. In the seventeenth century, John Amos

Comenius pointed out in Eastern Europe the role education could have in the advancement of peace (Harris, 2008). As a visionary theologian, he believed in the power of dreams. Maria Montessori (1992), his successor in Europe, witnessed a world war and articulated the crucial role of education in the advancement of global peace. She envisioned, and developed, a holistic approach to education that would cultivate the spiritual life of a child along with practical and intellectual skills. A part of Montessori pedagogy is aesthetics through learner experiences with beauty in the learning environment. That resonated with Immanuel Kant's notion of moral development (Kleingeld, 1999). While Kant (2003) advanced the idea that moral character can mature through exposure to the sublime, or greatness, Montessori demonstrated the positive outcomes of learning in a well-prepared and aesthetic setting. Such an environment fosters appreciation and cooperation between the people in it to preserve the beauty they perceive. Montessori's vision of intercultural cooperation started in the heterogeneous and multi-age class where children with various learning needs assisted each other in learning. She hoped their collaboration would foster peace in their adult lives.

Cooperative learning and conflict resolution in schools embody visions of people working together. Proponents and researchers of cooperative learning have also turned their attention to processes in schools that facilitate the resolution of conflicts (Johnson & Johnson, 1995). Elise Boulding advanced visions of a better world, which start with cooperative habits developed in the family and expand to local and global interactions. In *Building a Global Civic Culture* (1988a), Boulding points out that people use their imagination to solve problems. She went on to analyze the various uses and approaches to imagining before speculating why schools have not developed their students' imaging skills (Boulding, 1988b). From workshops that facilitated imaging, she found the following in the desirable futures the participants envisioned: "boundarylessness, multilinguality, equality, unity, sharing, clean environment, services for everyone" (p. 30). A core process of political as well as other contexts of peace development is the importance of imagining how transformation of conflict might occur (Galtung, 2004). Henry David Thoreau (1848) provided the notion of civil disobedience as a response to structural violence such as oppression. Mohandas Gandhi used that strategy with *satyagraha* to facilitate noncooperation with state oppression (Thoreau, 1848).

Several Westerners who had no direct experience with civil protest or war contemplated and described how education might promote peaceful interaction in society. John Dewey (1897) supported peace development via an education that emphasizes the current and future role of students in a democracy. He emphasized the importance of students having experiential education in their societies, in addition to pragmatic education in their classrooms. For that learning approach, he proposed that the teacher facilitate, versus direct, relevant experiences that best prepare each student for problem solving in the present as well as in the future (Dewey, 1897). While Dewey posited that experiential learning would benefit students and their community where they addressed problems, others claimed and demonstrated schools could do even more to reconstruct society. The notion of social reconstruction includes a viewpoint of education as the initiator of societal change for the better (Brameld, 1956/2010; Counts, 1932). Alvin Toffler (1974) and others advanced futuristic thinking about change. It is evident in the hope for societal improvement via education that stimulates problem solving. In that vein, Reardon (1988) advocated for education about human rights and the sources of rights violations. By incorporating different perspectives, such as gender lenses, educators can prepare students to analyze and respond to structural violence that they recognize (Reardon, 2001). Violence in schools is recognizable in multiple types of harm, whether or not there is bloodshed. Consequently, organizations have been providing lessons and other strategies for preventing and responding to violence (Constitutional Rights Foundation, 2013; Teaching Tolerance, 2013). Paulo Freire (1998) designed instruction that prepares people to recognize and proactively respond to oppression. He demonstrated how students addressed systemic conflict while they were also acquiring basic skills such as literacy. This method of reading the word and the world has been continued with the aid of teacher responsiveness and corresponding curriculum, which the organization Rethinking Schools and others provide (Christensen, 2003; Souto-Manning, 2009).

Critical pedagogy provides a foundation for anti-oppression education that includes identification of power differences in schools and their societies. Recognized are these differences in association with social dysfunctions stemming from racism, sexism, and the perpetuation of white privilege (Giroux, 1988). The awareness that critical pedagogy cultivates of these social, political, and economic problems corresponds with the development of worldview consciousness. Awareness of the lens used to view situations is a precursor to understanding interactions in a particular context. For example, listening to others describe or tell the story of a conflict demonstrates the role of perspective in relating events and evidences perception variation (Four Arrows & Mann, 2013; Yogev, 2010). The concept of worldview describes the overall perception of life. "Unity-based worldview" perceives the purpose of human life as the development and maintenance of peace (Danesh, 2008). This stage of worldview development follows the stages of survival-based worldview that young children and those in war zones often have, and then the identity-based worldview that characterizes adolescence and people in authoritarian circumstances. People of all ages may remain in the precursor categories to unity-based worldview. Social educators understand and respond to the worldviews of students with efforts to stimulate broader perceptions of reality and goals for life in it. One way of accomplishing this is orienting students to a world without violence. Resources of hope is an encompassing concept presented in *Educating Beyond Violent Futures* that describes processes as well as concrete aids for facilitating that orientation (Hutchinson, 1996, 2002). Such resources have included restorative practices, reconstruction projects, and educational aids for teaching about the current as well as historical peace development. Knowledge of as well as connection with projects that exist around the world for the advancement of peace provides a resource of hope that governments as well as nongovernmental organizations have been advancing.

Global synergies

This chapter identifies the combined international efforts to develop and maintain peace. The description will increase awareness of how others have applied the foundational notions. Examples of the theoretical enactments presented to students illustrate peace-oriented work. Teachers and students can analyze these efforts and discover how people, including school members, exhibit agency in their role as world citizens.

The Soka Gakkai, which translates from Japanese to English as the "Value Creation Society," is an international collaboration based in the traditions of Nichiren Buddhism. It has a "fundamental aim and mission of contributing to peace, culture and education based on the philosophy and ideals of the Buddhism of Nichiren Daishonin" (Soka Gakkai International, 2014). The Charter of the Soka Gakkai International (SGI) includes a focus on the future with a vision of peaceful coexistence wherein people have learned to resolve their conflicts without violence.

The principles of the Soka Gakkai (Table 1.2) resonate with the goals of the United Nations Educational, Scientific and Cultural Organization's Culture of Peace Campaign (2012). The International Decade for a Culture of Peace and Non-Violence for the Children of the World, launched in 2001, generated information about how the pursuit of peace through education and other means has been occurring around the world (Adams, 2005). During this Decade, awareness, including the advancement of peace education, became a resource of hope. That was needed information for teachers who have had to rationalize why they focused lessons on the skills of peace development and maintenance.

Several local as well as global organizations have been providing students venues for applying their skills in the pursuit of peace. For example, the World Social Forum (2002) affords opportunities for collaboration across the world for enactment of student agency. One of the organization's charter principles states: "The World Social Forum is a plural, diversified, non-confessional, non-governmental and non-party context that, in a decentralized fashion, interrelates organizations and movements engaged in concrete action at levels from the local to the international to build another world" (Principle 8). While the World

TABLE 1.2 *Purposes and principles of Soka Gakkai's Charter*

We, the constituent organizations and members of SGI, therefore, being determined to raise high the banner of world citizenship, the spirit of tolerance, and respect for human rights based on the humanistic spirit of Buddhism, and to challenge the global issues that face humankind through dialogue and practical efforts based on a steadfast commitment to nonviolence, hereby adopt this Charter, affirming the following purposes and principles:

- SGI shall contribute to peace, culture and education for the happiness and welfare of all humanity based on the Buddhist respect for the sanctity of life.
- SGI, based on the ideal of world citizenship, shall safeguard fundamental human rights and not discriminate against any individual on any grounds.
- SGI shall, based on the Buddhist spirit of tolerance, respect other religions, engage in dialogue and work together with them toward the resolution of fundamental issues concerning humanity.
- SGI shall respect cultural diversity and promote cultural exchange, thereby creating an international society of mutual understanding and harmony.
- SGI shall contribute to the promotion of education, in pursuit of truth as well as the development of scholarship, to enable all people to cultivate their individual character and enjoy fulfilling and happy lives.

(Adapted from the Charter of the Soka Gakkai International, 2014, para. 4.)

Social Forum promotes planning in regional and international meetings that students may travel to, Kids for Peace is an example of agency promotion for children in local settings. The commitment to peace development it facilitates orients them toward future and immediate engagement in caring (Noddings, 2008). The organization provides the Kids for Peace Pledge that states the following:

> I pledge to use my words to speak in a kind way.
> I pledge to help others as I go throughout my day.
> I pledge to care for our earth with my healing heart and hands.
> I pledge to respect people in each and every land.
> I pledge to join together as we unite the big and small.
> I pledge to do my part to create PEACE for one and all.
> (Kids for Peace, 2012, Pledge for Peace)

Multiple organizations that want students to know about and have skills for peace support peace-oriented social education research. For example, the Peace Education Commission of the International Peace Research Association brings together the research and researchers from nations around the world who examine education for peace and its outcomes. At the local level, there are regional organizations such as the Peace Education Special Interest Group of the American Educational Research Association in the USA. Articles many of these researchers publish in the *Journal of Peace Education* and several other bodies of literature support educational practices, such as teaching students, to envision a life characterized by peace.

Picturing peaceful lives

Having a picture of a possible situation expresses an idea. The idea of peace has been evident across illustrations humans have made as well as in thoughts they have expressed in speech and writing. The human need for peace has been associated with spirituality, psychology, and politics, which artists have documented in graphics and performance. More recently, educators who recognize the many dimensions of life that need attention in schools have proactively responded. While teachers and others are establishing a place and time for student learning about peace in schools, they need rationale due to the lack of inclusion this subject has had in the formal curriculum. Peace has been missing in standards for social education, which this book responds to elsewhere. The rationale has many sources, with the main one being the potential humans have for creating advancements in their world, after they picture a better situation.

Human nature provides a rationale. People find ways to manifest peace subsequent to their envisioning of it. The ability results from having an idea and freeing the mind and body to do that creative work. In her essay "Envisioning the Peaceable Kingdom," Elise Boulding (2000) identified the quadruple sets of human talent—mind, spirit, heart, and fantasy—for imagining peace and the conditions that support it. Through electronic media and printed literature, children of all ages are being exposed to fantasy that incorporates violence and normalizes it in the mind (Cortés, 2000). Youth and adults who consume such media have active fantasies about violence. Converting their experiences with fantasy for an orientation toward peace is not only possible, it is comforting. For example, my own children of varying ages have been choosing not to watch media with violence. They know it has scary effects on themselves, stimulating nightmares about how conflicts can turn violent and hinder social intelligence. They tell me how senseless the plot of a program or book they encounter is when it presents characters using violence in response to conflict. When I ask them what the character might have done to solve the problem without violence, they typically think of multiple means and then identify one they think would be best.

Examples of peaceful responses to conflict are not emphasized enough, if at all, in the typical curriculum of education. Consequently, there is a need for incorporating conflict analysis across the curriculum. Young people would benefit from knowing the rich record of nonviolent conflict resolution that humans have. That awareness can build a sense of control. Young people who have less feelings of control about the future are more likely to engage in and be victims of violence (Galinsky & Salmond, 2002). Hence, concepts of control, such as those articulated by Starhawk (1987), "power-over, power-from-within and power-with," have been useful in teaching for hope (de los Reyes & Gozemba, 2002, p. 12). The "imagination-intellect" that Weems (2003) describes is a skill that allows construal of the "not yet," which Maxine Greene (1995) recommended as an instructional concept. Along with that, having knowledge of how humans have accomplished peace in the past can advance the skill of picturing conflict resolution without violence.

TABLE 1.3 *Visioning as curriculum*

Subject	Contents
Writing	Vocabulary and genres for stating peace concepts and development
Literacy	Predictions of conflicts in stories as peacefully resolved
Social Studies	Multicultural history and "herstory" of peace after envisioning
Science	Developments for needs for multiple species, as well as humans
Math	Multiple systems and their applications for problem solving
Health	Treatment and prevention of health threats
Arts	Venues and diverse means of expressing peace possibilities

Across the curriculum in schools, students can learn how to envision. Within the social studies, art, music, and literature, students can acquire information and express their ideas, especially those that words do not easily convey (Bae, 2012; Eisner, 1991). For example, the teacher Sabrina Thornton (2007) designed a lesson for student engagement with futurism by expressing in response to conflicts via cardboard sculptures. Beyond social education, a cross-curricular presentation enhances the relevance and coherence of a concept, such as the future. Throughout all subject lessons, students can develop the skill of picturing a better situation. Table 1.3 identifies spaces in subject areas for such instruction. Ian Harris and Mary Lee Morrison (2013, pp. 121–123) provide a more elaborated list of examples for Infusing Peace and Justice Concepts into School Curricula.

Inclusion is a method of integration that makes spaces across subject areas for more than envisioning need fulfillment. It also enables learning about and through different perspectives. Including diverse perspectives can provide a record of human accomplishments across contexts, cultures, genders, ages, social classes, and ability characteristics. Such inclusion can help people envision a more peaceful world. The role of visions in rendering a better situation is apparent when students learn about its effects as a response to conflict. Including the accounts of that process across continents in ancient to modern times helps students understand, for instance, how goal setting, galvanizing, and mobilizing for change without violence has been a continual opportunity. The psychological effects associated with inclusive visioning, following an experience with violence, are healing, connecting, and empowering. Opportunities in the community for seeing and engaging in visioning add relevance to school curriculum.

Countless organizations around the world have visions of peace. Information about their projects is available in print and electronic literature, from basic knowledge of the visions to critical analysis of them. For example, the organization International Cities of Peace (2012) provides definitions, examples, and resources for construing and enacting "cities of imagination." Students can relevantly incorporate, in each of their subject areas, information this organization features about developing peace in a city. In tandem with their investigation of visions that other people have, students use art to illustrate what they envision as peace.

The arts support many aspects of social education. Through examination of illustrations, students learn about expressions of conflict and responses to it. Exposing them to illustrations and performances about peace visions and peace development enacts social as well as artistic goals of education. Precursors of peacemaking have been portrayal and performance techniques. By producing art along with observation and analysis, thoughts about life without violence take form and facilitate communication (Read, 1949; Shank & Schirch, 2008). Without expressions of possibilities, it is difficult to manifest peace in violent situations. Educational psychologists use art produced by students to analyze how the learners experience life and develop their capabilities for managing conflict. When harmed by violence, the arts can be therapeutic as well as useful for student learning (Scharf & Bhagat, 2007). Clearly, arts in education are deep and wide like an ocean with waves that carry ashore nutrients and wash away the tracks of conflict in the shifting sands of lives. Peace education contextually responds to such changes, which shape the curriculum teachers infuse with current social situations as relevant content.

Goals of peace education

The goals of peace education illustrate visions of life without violence and hopes for human manifestation of it (Fisk, 2000). The main goal "is to provide images of peace, so that when people are faced with conflict, they will choose to be peaceful" (Harris & Morrison, 2013, p. 29). Although conceptions of peace and culturally appropriate ways of bringing it about are diverse, there are commonalities in those visions that exist as universal goals. Globally evident are themes of improved human relations, preventing violence as a response to conflict, and stewardship. Students experience these themes in visionary learning as preparation for avoidance of harm in response to conflict within and between societies. Development of student capabilities with skills that have been useful in problem solving is another goal of peace education. With a reduction of time spent on review of wars, lessons can include topics that foster thinking about future as well as past and present challenges in bringing about peace (Salazar, 1995). For example, how people might better relate to each other, and other species, is a challenge of human relations.

Education about improved human relations occurs through student analysis of interactions. In the lessons about continuity and change, picturing better relationships within and between communities helps to address goals for harmonious interactions. This includes integration, collaboration, and cooperation with displays of respect and cross-cultural honoring. Students can identify needed changes in a community with their possible roles in the present as well as future improvements. Making changes without harm is a key component of those accomplishments.

Change without harm entails creativity. Humans have a fantastic record of problem solving through the continual creation of tools. Recognition of how inventions have enabled adaptation to existing and changing environments leads to the awareness that humans can broadly facilitate creativity for problem solving. With this knowledge, the goal of ending violence as a response to conflicts in different contexts is not lofty. It is as practical as tool invention and as crucial as survival. Ending violence is a commitment that requires knowledge and skills for creation of solutions in three domains of conflict: intrapersonal, interpersonal, and systemic.

Students learn about sources of conflicts and unmet needs in each of the three domains that Table 1.4 provides. A comprehensive study of conflict reveals how the three domains have causal relationships. Students see how the inner life of a person affects the way one relates to others and that those relations can impact the society, nation, and world. They are ripple effects. For example, they learn how Mohandas Gandhi used great self-control when he was treated violently in South Africa as an Indian attorney, and then how he creatively responded with others to the structural conflict of ethnic discrimination. His recommendation for individuals to do the inner work of first addressing their personal needs was a directive for accomplishing intrapersonal peace. Self-care is not a precursor to work in the interpersonal and systemic domains of conflict. Rather, evident conflicts and needs in each domain necessitate constructive responses in tandem. Powerful social education demonstrates that success in each area affects the ability to harmlessly work for conflict solutions in the other domains. Succeeding involves work in the mind of each individual, the relationships with others, and structures in society (Purkey, 2000). Envisioning a peaceful future includes the skill of picturing how people interact with themselves and with others to fulfill needs. Sustaining such interactions can lead to transformation whereas solving a conflict in just one domain is resolution. Without addressing the other domains, especially the fulfillment of life-sustaining needs, there is not a transformation of conflict. This is evident in the same as well as in the other domains it affects. Managing human impact in the biological well-being of the world involves all three aspects of conflict transformation.

Biological and social stewardship is a sense of responsibility for the natural environment as well as for people (Lin & Oxford, 2011). This value takes expression through recognition of plant and animal life as interdependent with people, who through their creative abilities can work for preservation and well-being. With concern about human interactions beyond the planet, such as leaving nuclear waste in outer space, the notion of this disposition as "planetary stewardship" expands to incorporate galactic responsibility (Wenden, 2004). While perceiving the universe's components in an immense web of interdependence, this broader view accounts for the role of the earth and its inhabitants as one (Berry, 1984; Kimura, 2009). Entertainment media commonly presents images of interaction in outer space as violent, thereby causing an expectation for harm beyond as well as on the planet. Comprehensive visions of peace and commitments to the work for bringing it about can counter the normalization of violence in near and far places. For instance, the Earth Charter promotes social and ecological justice. Its signatories agree to include the rights of all humans and other life forms as considerations when evaluating the possible or evident impact of human effects on nature and the need of people for livable conditions (Earth Charter Initiative, 2012). In evaluation of eco-justice, students learn to analyze consumption and construction as well as destructive

TABLE 1.4 *Domains of conflict transformation*

Domain	Characteristics
Intrapersonal	Self-awareness and management: thought processes, inner voice, emotions
Interpersonal	Relationships and interactions with others
Systemic/structural	Systems and social structures that sustain conflict

behaviors. Awareness of how consumption choices impact the producers of those goods and the environment enables student evaluation of their own social and ecological footprints (Oxford, 2011). This lens focuses on more than "equitable distribution of Earth's resources within sustainable limits of natural systems" (Mische & Harris, 2012, p. 6). It also brings into the picture of peace social inequities, which result in biological harm to humans and nature. Students develop analytical skills for biological and social stewardship that have applications in many situations.

Visionary education seeks development of knowledge, skills, and dispositions associated with advancement of peace. Social education includes several of those capabilities. Practice with analysis skills occurs across subject contexts because conflict as a topic appears in every discipline of study (Table 1.6). Students analyze the antecedents of intrapersonal and interpersonal as well as structural conflict. They use analysis for identification of their own psychological needs when they detect, through their emotions or actions, evidence of intrapersonal conflict. More recently, Elias and Arnold (2006) describe the cultivation of this skill as social and emotional learning. That skill development in social education shows a vision of youth and future adults who can manage their conflicts without harming anyone. Presentation of situations that skillfully avoid violence in peace history provides a knowledge base for understanding and accomplishing nonviolence (Table 1.7). Nonfiction for students of all ages enables learning of peace history (Carter & Picket, 2014). For

TABLE 1.5 *Capability goals*

Capability	Evidence
Positive self-concept	Healthy self-esteem
Acceptance of diversity	Accommodation and cultivation
Values clarification and moral responsibility	Personal, family, cultural, societal, and global beliefs that underlie peaceful living
Emotions management	Recognizing, naming, and handling
Considerate communication	Thoughtfully expressing needs and requests
Hearing to understand	Active listening with all senses for expressed needs
Analysis of needs	Identification of life-sustaining requirements
Cognitive complexity	Flexibility and higher-order thinking
Empowerment	Feeling capable of making positive transformation
Stewardship	Protection
Problem-solving strategies	Positive (harmless) approaches
Restoration	Reconstruction where there is damage
Reconciliation	Build healthy connections with former disputants
Action orientation	Facilitation of and participation in problem solving
Employment	Identification of jobs and careers in peace development

Foundations of Social Education for Peace

TABLE 1.6 *Case example*

Dramatic Performances that Demonstrate Peace

Before there is a performance to create peace, there must be a story to perform. High school teacher Mary Maio assigned each student in her Digital Media Class development of a story that had peaceful resolution of the conflict the plot featured. After rewriting the story into a screenplay, there was the opportunity for performance of it in front of a camera. Local student film festivals, international film festivals, the local cable channel, the cable station's Internet channel, and YouTube screened the students' completed productions. The writing of the story and screenplay production took one semester.

The overall goal of the assignment was to write for production of a short film that demonstrates how teenagers might proactively respond to conflict. Situations in their lives typically characterized by violence were the topics of their stories. Throughout the assignment, Mary Maio wrote in her reflection journal about how most of the students lacked knowledge of ways for transforming conflict into a positive experience for all involved. As a result, she designed a curriculum that included strategies for peacefully responding to conflicts. Her curriculum included the following activities:

1. Reading daily the words posted on the wall in large letters: Everyone has talent. Everyone has talent to create peace
2. Identifying positive and negative self-talk
3. Modeling compassionate communication skills
4. Applying conflict resolution skills for the purpose of compromising
5. Identifying and expressing feelings
6. Visual journaling: "Going Deeper Than Words" activity to reduce stress, reduce anger, and envision peace
7. Applying media literacy skills: using techniques in creating fear, anger, hate, and peace
8. Participating in writers' meetings: students arranged in small groups to share their stories and to help each other in identifying how to make their plots more peaceful
9. Building a body of work to give a sense of accomplishment of purposeful work
10. Laughing and enjoying the process

Example: Going Deeper Than Words Activity

Take a few deep breaths and imagine what peace feels like. Allow yourself to feel inside your body. Notice the air going in and out of your body. Sense any area that feels most alive and where the energy flows freely, warm and relaxed. Next, imagine what this physical sensation would look like in an image. When you feel comfortable with an image of peace, color, scribble, or sketch a picture of peace.

By the end of the school year, Ms. Maio (2007) noted that the students were amazed at their ability to develop ways for peacefully resolving conflicts in their own lives.

example, the story "Rice for Peace" published in 13 languages describes a peace campaign that influenced President Eisenhower (Canfield et al., 2005). Additionally, awareness of reconciliation facilitations in different contexts, involving connections between former disputants and combatants, adds more details in the pictures of peacemaking students' minds. The diverse ways in which those facilitations of peace have happened illustrate the value of using locally developed strategies that incorporate the norms of the involved population. Table 1.5 lists several other capabilities that peace-oriented social education promotes.

Conclusion

Philosophical stepping stones from around the world and the time span of humanity provide the multi-dimensional foundation of visionary social education. Construal of peace has been evident in the spiritual, ethical, and theoretical expressions of culture. Available through not only the arts, but also the curriculum of peace-oriented social education and resources teachers can access are modern descriptions of peace notions. The integration of peace as a topic for picturing the future exists as an opportunity for infusion of social education across the subject areas. When students learn about past, present, and future peace, there are three dimensions of conflict with which students can practice their skills: intrapersonal processes, interpersonal relations, and structural challenges. The capability goals include use of knowledge about peace processes of the past and present for resolution and transformation of conflict as well as for envisioning a future without violence. On this

TABLE 1.7 Lesson plan

Playwriting about Peace
Lesson Goal Students will know and enact visionary responses to conflicts that past and current leaders have managed.
Exploration Students describe their awareness of how leaders, including change makers who were not politicians, have expressed or used visions of peaceful communities, nations, and the world.
Development Students collect information from literature, interviews of community members, and performing as well as graphic arts they can examine directly or indirectly in media about the visions leaders have described in their work to resolve conflict.
Expansion Students create a fictional play for a performance in the school, along with a bulletin board, marquis, and fliers to advertise it, about a visionary leader who accomplished social and environmental peace with the help of others in bringing about that vision.

multi-dimensional foundation, teachers have used the arts and literature for visionary learning while they accomplished cross-curricular learning objectives that include those of social education. When they offered and enabled opportunities for students' proactive responses to structural conflict, they fostered agency needed in a democracy to facilitate change without harm. That is the foundation for global citizenship.

Instruction opportunities. Teach students about prosocial responses to conflict that people throughout time and around the world have made. Present ideas in different spiritual and indigenous traditions that demonstrate the ways humans have thought about and envisioned peace. Include current initiatives that have international participation in pursuit of peace. Facilitate visioning aspects of peace in each subject area for students. Enable student practice with the three domains of conflict transformation that are useful for avoidance of harm.

Curricular applications

1. Plan for student contemplation of good societies. They can consider precepts and principles from different thought traditions. They can also clarify the values that help them decide what is good. Make available precepts and principles from different cultures and faiths. Consider the precepts that leaders in the student's society used. Give students opportunities for expression of their contemplation through multiple modalities.
2. Have students identify precepts and principles of different cultures that they recognize as related. These might be expressed in charts and artistic depictions or dramas that combine common notions.
3. Facilitate student recognition of values that characters in fiction and real people in nonfiction enacted. Have them identify multiple resources where the characters may have acquired those values in their communities.
4. Enable anonymous descriptions by students of harms that happen on their campus. Share these observations with other campus members in a collective pursuit of harm elimination. Encourage creativity in generation of ideas about harm avoidance.
5. Assist students in identification of a need in their community that affects intrapersonal and interpersonal interactions.

6 Develop an opportunity in each subject area for student expression of visions. Invite inclusion of a process or way of living that illustrates peace.
7 Design a checklist without quantitative indicators for student progress on the Capability Goals that Table 1.5 of this chapter displays. Use it for monthly monitoring of student development. Plan developmental experiences that will aid student learning in any areas of weakness.

Resources for visionary learning

On the Internet

Artists Culture of Peace (http://www.sgi-usa.org/newsandevents/exhibitions/ArtistsAsPeacemakers-Web-Dec07.pdf)
The Earth Charter (http://www.earthcharterinaction.org/content/pages/Read-the-Charter.html)
Futurism Cardboard Sculpture (http://sabrinasbest.tripod.com/id28.html)
The Great Peace...The Gathering of Good Minds. CD-ROM (http://www.greatpeace.org/)
Heroes for a Better World (http://www.doonething.org/heroes/heroes-z.htm)
Journal of Stellar Peacemaking (http://74.127.11.121/peacejournal/index.html)
Peace 4 Turtle Island (http://www.peace4turtleisland.org/) provides information about each of the six nations of the Haudenosaunee through interaction with the depicted Aiionwatha Belt that documented their history.
This includes the history, culture, and spirituality of the Haudenosaunee (Six Nations Iroquois League), including the Great Law of Peace they created and use as a guide for living.

Literature

Adler, D. A. (2007). *Heroes for civil rights*. New York, NY: Holiday House Books.
Bausum, A. (2004). *With courage and cloth: Winning the fight for a woman's right to vote*. Washington, DC: National Geographic Children's Books.
Canfield, J., Hansen, M. V., Carter, C. C., Palomares, S., Williams, L. K., & Winch, B. L. (eds) (2005). *Chicken soup for the soul: Stories for a*

better world. Deerfield Beach, FL: Health Communications. Available at http://chickensoup.peacestories.info/

Capaldi, G. (2008). *A boy named Beckoning: The true story of Dr. Carlos Montezuma, Native American hero*. Minneapolis, MN: Carolrhoda Books.

Caravantes, P. (2004). *Waging peace: The story of Jane Addams*. Greensboro, NC: Morgan Reynolds.

Fournel, K. (2007) *Great women from our first nations*. Toronto, ON, Canada: Second Story.

Freedman, R. (2006). *Freedom Walkers: The story of the Montgomery Bus Boycott*. New York: Holiday House.

Krull, K. (2003). *Harvesting hope: The story of Cesar Chavez*. San Diego, CA: Harcourt Children's Books.

Lasky, K. (2006). *John Muir: America's first environmentalist*. Cambridge: Candlewick.

Pinkney, A. (2000). *Let it shine: Stories of black women freedom fighters*. Singapore: Gulliver.

Weatherford, C. B. (2007). *Freedom on the menu: The Greensboro sit-ins*. New York, NY: Puffin.

Wilson, J. (2008). *One peace: True stories of young activists*. Victoria, British Columbia, Canada: Orca.

Winter, J. (2008). *Wangari's trees of peace: A true story from Africa*. New York, NY: Houghton Mifflin.

Zalben, J. B. (2006). *Paths to peace: People who changed the world*. New York, NY: Dutton.

Glossary

Affective education: identification and awareness of feelings involving social and emotional literacy.

Agency: the knowledge and ability to act for collective as well as individual betterment.

Circles: group meetings formed as circles that convey membership equality in problem-solving communication and restoration following harm.

Civil disobedience: noncooperation with the state for bringing attention to the ways it sustains structural conflict or violence.

Critical pedagogy: anti-oppression education that recognizes and proactively responds to power differences in schools and their societies.

e Munthu: (Malawian language) humanness, the qualities and capabilities of humanity.

Proactive: the motivation to be active in response to recognized needs.

Prosocial: an orientation toward improvement of society through conscientious interactions in it.

Satyagraha: insistence for truth while being steadfast in revealing and proactively responding to structural conflict or violence.

Social and ecological footprint: the impact of social and biological behaviors.

Surface culture: the behavioral norms and customs of a culture, in contrast with deep culture, which is the values and beliefs that partially influence the peoples' behaviors.

The Way (*Tao*): precepts that guide principled life choices.

Expansion

1. Describe multiple examples of peace visions in your world region during the past millennia. What have people in your area identified as visions that evidence the state of peace? How have they used these visions?
2. Describe different artworks, including graphic and performing arts, that have expressed visions of peace or harmless processes for bringing it about. Identify any that one could use for stimulation and expression of peace visions where you are. You can find artwork online if there is not any available in a local collection.
3. In your current community and school, describe how the goals of peace-oriented education have been advanced. How are students developing related knowledge and skills?
4. Reflect on your foundations for peace. List ideas, theories, and values that support your efforts to have peace. Explain how you demonstrate your efforts in your daily activities.
5. How might you facilitate visions of peaceful futures with the notions from different cultures and world regions of peaceful living? Provide examples of ways to facilitate these visions both in and out of the school environment.
6. Make a plan to incorporate opportunities for student development of capabilities within your instructional practices. How might you implement ideas and suggestions described in this chapter? For example, which foundational notions could you identify in literature students read or arts they can analyze? What depicted visions of the future exhibit the condition of peace?

2
Peace-Focused Policy for Social Education

Abstract: *Visions are catalysts for change that policy facilitates. People with a vision embodied in education policy use the recommended strategies. Selection and usage of standards that support their visions are contemporary responses to policy. Contextually, responsive usage of policy can reflect critical analysis of the prescribed instruction. Social reconstructionism and cognitive constructivism are two theories that underlie policy responses and progressive pedagogy. State policies that recommend instruction in conflict management or social and emotional literacy demonstrate visions of peace. This chapter provides a case example of progressive state policies along with Standards for Peace Education.*

Carter, Candice C. *Social Education for Peace: Foundations, Teaching, and Curriculum for Visionary Learning.* New York: Palgrave Macmillan, 2015.
DOI: 10.1057/9781137534057.0006.

Documentation, endorsement, and adoption of visions can be catalysts for change when they result in policies. Policy is an official agreement to pursue a course of action based on one or more established goals. Peace-focused policy in the field of education can have wide-ranging effects depending on the breadth of policy adoption and the readiness of those positioned for policy implementation. People who share the vision embodied in the policy may engage in its enactment, unless they face structural constraints (Charalambous, Charalambous, & Zemblas, 2013). However, the knowledge and skills they have, as well as their efficacy, will often limit their actions (DePaul, 2010). Feeling capable of accomplishing a goal is efficacy. Preparation is crucial to use of visionary policy. Therefore, policy for peace-focused social education includes recommendations for preparation of those who will enact the policy.

Policies, standards, and guidelines differ in the level of their adoption. When recommendations are mandated, they become policy. Standards for education become policy when there is a requirement for their use in planning instruction. Guidelines are recommendations that an organization produces to influence practice. In the field of education, guidelines are often contained within a provided curriculum. Teachers can also find guidelines in topic-related literature that offers recommendations for practice. The influence of standards and guidelines is more variable if not mandated in policy. Using standards or guidelines has both positive and negative results.

Selection and usage

When educators value their professional autonomy to select instructional methods that align with their current pedagogical practices, that can seem best for their students' learning success, and a requirement to use different instruction may not result in transformation of their practices. Resistance is one identified response to standards-based educational reform while another is superficial use of the directives (Vinson, Ross, & Wilson, 2012). Without first developing vision of and commitment to the change, superficial efforts to accomplish or resistance to the mandate can result. The emotional response of teachers during a policy change influences its implementation. This is especially the case if the new policy feels threatening to teachers (Smit, 2003). For example, there were different perceptions of and responses to directives for socially just education that lacked clarity (Thrupp & Tomlinson, 2005). Through a vision of peace-promoting education, contextually responsive teaching, which policy supports, occurred (New York State Education Department, 2011).

Overcoming implementation constraints

Educators have developed selection strategies to limit the amount of required guidelines they will use when facing a multitude of standards for instructional planning. One method teachers have used for consideration of policy is ranking of the mandated standards by common priorities for instruction (Reeves, 2002). This process of identifying the "power standards" that some educators perceive as most important in a prescribed set typically focuses on tested knowledge and skills (Chittenden Central Supervisory Union, 2015). However, that selection lacks a broad vision for educational outcomes when it focuses on success with narrowed instruction. For example, social studies tests of student learning typically require recall of events with the limited perspective of dominant culture (those with power) about what happened. These recalled events included in tests are more often military engagements than diplomacy interactions that resolved social and political conflicts without violence. Unless a vision of unity and peace aid the selection process for "power standards," social education will be unable to support transformative instruction that equips students with the knowledge, skills, and dispositions they need for achieving that goal. In identification of "power standards," the value of teaching for and about peace needs to be evident.

Another constraint to adoption of prescribed standards is differential valuing based on association of each standard with the subject matter that educators know well and are accustomed to teaching (Butroyd, 2001). In this reduction approach, teachers select the standards that align best with the values they teach in one or more subject areas where they feel comfortable providing instruction. Consequently, usage limitations of standards occur when teachers do not feel a need for, or confidence with, those that connect social education with other content areas. For example, it is more common to value gender balance in lessons about her story/history in social studies, but less common in science lessons where female contributions to technical and other types of discoveries and development need to be included. Teachers may also lack the value, in this case for gender balance, due to their lack of prior exposure to such values in education. This situation evidences the importance of developing professional values for, and confidence with, the breadth of content that standards prescribe. It also highlights the need for educators to consider particular as well as general factors that influence their instruction. While thinking about which standards to use, conscientious teachers take into account the cultural context of their students, such as values and corresponding norms, along with the associated needs their pupils have evidenced. Those considerations include goals that are particular to the students' cultures. For example, when I taught students whose parents were members of the armed forces at a nearby military base, I was keenly aware of the need to show the value of respect for the roles their parents had as government agents. When teaching about international conflict and the role of government in peacemaking, the lessons included the roles the students' parents had as agents of peace—watching out for the safety of people who were in the region of the conflict. This stimulated student communication with their military parents about what their work involved. Military parents continually expressed their appreciation for this inclusion in social studies of current conflicts and their roles in them. One parent told me, "Nobody wants peace more than us [military], and I am so glad you are teaching about how it has happened [peace history]." None of these parents complained when they saw documentation on television of my involvement in civic action to avoid an international war. They likely understood my effort to encourage nonviolent responses to the current international conflict and recognized the value of my actions as civic involvement, which the Peace Education Standard for disposition development supports (see Appendix). Ultimately, contextual factors beyond teachers' subject interests and values are determinants of standards selection and facilitation.

Standards of complexity

The term "standards of complexity" encapsulates this idea of contextually responsive usage (Kincheloe, 2001). A foundation of this notion is elimination in education of reductionism, fragmentation, and abstract individualism that can limit the depth and breadth of learning. The canon of knowledge, which many government-mandated standards reinforce, becomes flexible with standards of complexity. Information is not reduced to merely that which policy identifies, which fragments curriculum and bypasses some students' cultural backgrounds along with the current contexts of their lives. In avoidance of reductionism with standards that simply reinforce the information creators of mandated guidelines had, standards of complexity are contextually responsive. Concerns that rationalize standards of complexity include: (a) the limitations of ethnocentric perspectives, (b) lack of student participation in knowledge production, and (c) biases inherent in technical rationality that hamper achievement success along class, culture, and gender lines. With standards that allow accommodation and use of the contextual conditions, which influence learning, education is more likely to foster the development of "sophisticated, ethical and visionary knowledge workers" (Kincheloe, 2001, p. 41). Such human characteristics have supported peaceful transformation of society. Two foundational facets of education, social reconstructionism and cognitive constructivism, support the development of those capacities.

Social reconstructionism and cognitive constructivism

Two theories woven together provide a placemat for visionary education at the policy table. In Chapter 1, a discussion of social reconstructionism demonstrated the visionary thrust of that ideology. Working in tandem with a theory of cognitive development, social reconstructionism provides a heuristic for progressive pedagogy. Teaching for cognitive constructivism accommodates student schema, which is their pre-existing knowledge, in a process approach to learning. Constructivist social education occurs in three developmental phases that comprise a progression of learning. These three stages of learning and lesson planning are exploration, development, and expansion. They comprise the learning cycle. For example, constructivist learning begins in the exploration phase with exploration of students' conceptions. Following that information-gathering stage, a teacher prepares the developmental phase of the learning cycle that responds to students' ideas and beliefs about the lesson topic. In the developmental phase of their learning, students share and discover new ways that the concept is evident. The students also find culturally relevant information the teacher includes in the lesson with awareness of their backgrounds (Fitchett & Heafner, 2012). In this second phase of the learning cycle, students construct a broader repertoire of knowledge and skills, which when applied, can reshape their dispositions associated with the concept. During the third phase of the learning cycle, students apply their knowledge and skills through expansion of those developments. For social reconstruction, students can learn in a constructivist lesson about compassionate communication that enables hearing about unmet needs.

We see in Table 2.1 how the lesson plan incorporates student schema by first allowing them to brainstorm about the focus topic. The teacher uses the students' conceptions to subsequently design their developmental experiences and plan for expansion activities in which they may practice their new skills. For example, a teacher of young children created a multicultural arts curriculum and whole-group discussions after she observed the anti-social discourse of her pupils in exploratory activities (Silva & Langhout, 2011). After the development stage, the students practiced their revised descriptions of diverse populations and helped each other in that process. The construction of learning begins within the contexts of the students' lives. It incorporates their initial concepts and experiences for planning their learning development and subsequently expands to applications in different situations. In the expansion phase, students see how techniques may vary across cultural contexts for accommodation of cultural and personal differences. As part of their cognitive construction, they develop acceptance of norm variation in communication styles as well as the ability to use them. In the example shown in Table 2.2, students learn in the expansion phase of the lesson to code switch, which is a change in language style, while maintaining compassionate messages for problem solving.

The lesson includes communication techniques that have been very useful for peacemaking (Rosenberg, 2000). Policy which supports contextually responsive instruction and cognitive construction is a foundation for change that results from articulated visions by those who see possibilities for improving conditions of life. It can support social reconstruction.

TABLE 2.1 *Compassionate communication lesson with the learning cycle*

Lesson Phase	Content
Exploration	Brainstorm to collect students' ideas of meaning and skills
Development	Clarify their known communication techniques and teach others
Expansion	Use techniques in different cultural contexts to transform conflicts

TABLE 2.2 Code-switching activity with compassionate communication

Procedure	Student pairs take various identity roles to orally ask the same question in the appropriate communication style for that relationship. After each role-play, observers provide feedback on the practice interactions and suggestions for cultural styles
Roles	Core Question "Are you feeling upset?"
Southern Friends	"Hey [referent or name], are you feeling upset?"
Child/parent	"Mother [or name], are you feeling upset?"
Student/teacher	"Teacher [or name], are you feeling upset?"
Driver/police	"Officer [or name], are you feeling upset?"
Citizen/president	"Madam President, are you feeling upset?"
Strangers	"Are you feeling upset?"

Foundations of peace-focused policies

In the meso context, recommendations for the development of peace through education have been available from international organizations. The foundations laid by such organizations support local as well as global efforts to provide peace education. During this time in human history, access to guidelines produced outside of the local region have enabled their consideration and use in other regions where there has been recognition of the need for such support. With the aid of access to information exchange, one can find and use global as well as local guidelines after interpreting and customizing them for current needs. What follows in this chapter is a brief review of initiatives that have provided foundational support to peace-focused social education.

Endorsements of peace education

Conventions and manifestos

Intended for global usage are endorsements of peace through education. Such clarion calls include the Hague Appeal for Peace (2000), the Decade for Peace, Resolution 53/25 (UNESCO, 1998), the Earth Charter (The Earth Charter Initiative, 2012), the Convention on Children's Rights (United Nations, 1989), and the Culture of Peace Resolution 52/13 of the United Nations (United Nations General Assembly, 1998). These resolutions by international policy organizations show urgency for development of universal as well as local peace initiatives. The policies are foundations on which nations and states can build regional capacities for peace education. This has occurred in varying degrees.

Ratified for enactment in almost every nation is the United Nations Convention on the Rights of the Child (1989). Governments that endorsed the protection of children's rights opened the door to many essential aspects of care which children have lacked. The reluctance in the USA to ratify the United Nations Convention on the Rights of the Child has evidenced a great need for attention to the problem of not only providing peace education for children, but also other aspects of living that children need for their future well-being. Without the adoption in the USA of the United Nations Convention on the Rights of the Child, there is a need for other forms of peace commitment. Schools have considered the importance of the Earth Charter (Earth Charter Initiative) and the conversion of resource waste to sustainable practices that occurs in them. Recognition by governments of the climate changes the earth is undergoing has been an impetus to the implementation of the Earth Charter. The declaration of United Nations for a Culture of Peace stimulated initiatives at local levels, especially in areas of recent armed conflict (Iram, Wahrman, & Gross, 2006). Regional commitments to peace-focused education have aligned with the UN recommendations in those locations. Schools of all levels and their governing bodies that have peace in their mission statements follow the Hague Appeal for Peace (2000). It recommends constructive problem solving. The Tirana Call for Peace Education, which ministers of education from several countries signed, recognized the value of education programs that aligned with the Hague Appeal for Peace (2004). Government support for peace-focused education has been a crucial catalyst for conversion of violence.

Statutes and mandates

Endorsements of peace-focused social education that governments have advanced increased the breadth of the practice as well as the depth of developments for its implementation. Many of the mandates for peace-focused education have been associated throughout the world with citizenship education. For example, Colombia has citizenship criteria which include knowledge and skills with the following education standards: coexistence, peace, and plurality (Ministerio de Educación Nacional Republic de Colombia, 2004). Learning to live with culturally different neighbors has been a challenge in many regions, especially where cross-cultural violence has occurred. The post-war program in the Federation of Bosnia and Herzegovina, called Education for Peace, had widespread applications with the support of government adoption and external funding. Applicable worldwide is the concept of unity through diversity that Education for Peace advances (Education for Peace, n.d.). Prime Minister Order Number 187/2003 in Thailand promotes study about how to peacefully respond to conflict (Ohio Commission on Dispute Resolution and Conflict Management, 2004). In Northern Ireland, the state policy of Education for Mutual Understanding (EMU) supported initiatives for all ages of children and teacher education (Carter, 2004a). While the great flexibility of the policy encouraged teachers to find their own ways of responding to pervasive sectarianism in the region, its lack of specificity in recommending best practices, and when to use them, resulted in less than optimal implementation (Gallagher, 2005; Smith & Robinson, 1996). Typical responses limited cross-community contact arrangements for students. Nevertheless, while the policy was in place, educators in Northern Ireland who created prosocial activities for accomplishing Education for Mutual Understanding evidenced a common vision of peace in their state through intercultural and cross-community harmony. The Ontario Ministry of Education in Canada (Naylor, 2008) funded recommendations that advanced organizational development of education for peace, but it did not translate into state policy. Consequently, the small support had a limited, but important effect—advancement of peace-focused education that became more widely available for adoption. Governmental support for peace-focused education is typically associated with the work of nongovernmental organizations (NGOs). A symbiotic relationship exists between the two types of institutions in that progress; one type is often the catalyst for developments by the other. Government statutes mirror recommendations by NGOs that specialize in social relations and education. Government grants partially sustain the work that NGOs undertake for peace development. A sampling of government standards in two states shown in Table 2.3 reveals the peace-related responsibilities articulated in two subject areas. It reveals the concept of nonviolence as an aspect of healthy behavior. In the subject of social studies, standards demonstrate the notion of a good citizen as one who can resolve conflict and improve society.

TABLE 2.3 *Case example*

State Standards
Health Education Standards California Department of Education (2008) Standard 4: Interpersonal Communication Describe ways to manage interpersonal conflicts nonviolently (p. 39) Standard 5: Decision Making Analyze the benefits of using nonviolent means to resolve conflicts (p. 21) Standard 7: Practicing Health-Enhancing Behaviors Practice ways to resolve conflicts nonviolently (p. 29) Florida Department of Education (2008) Standard 3 Responsible Behavior Demonstrate nonviolent strategies to manage or resolve conflict (p. 4)
Social Studies Standards Florida Department of Education (2008) Standard K.C.2.2 Demonstrate that conflicts among friends can be resolved in ways that are consistent with being a good citizen (p. 1) Standard 5.C.2.5 Identify ways good citizens go beyond basic civic and political responsibilities to improve government and society (p. 11) Standard 7.C.2.14 Conduct a service project to further the public good (p. 17) California History-Social Science Standards At the time of this book development, California did not have the words "nonviolence/nonviolent" in their standards for this subject area (California Department of Education, 2014).

Cross-organizational support

Institutions that generate recommendations for social education have an important task in advancing visionary education for peace. Ministries of Education in West Africa have benefited from the work of local NGOs such as the West Africa Network for Peace building (WANEP). The educational work of WANEP (2013) has contributed to the inclusion of peace-focused education in school programs and teacher preparation in that region. In war-torn Sierra Leone, the National Commission for Basic Education launched teacher-training modules in peace education while several NGOs supported such initiatives in the region. In Hiroshima and Nagasaki, city government and the organization Mayors for Peace have supported peace studies in Japan as well as in the USA.

While NGOs and other organizations that focus on social education may be located in one region, their recommendations and other forms of support can be far reaching for those who have access to international communications for information sharing. Consequently, recommendations made by organizations in one nation are considerations for use in another, although with apprehension on the part of educators who are unfamiliar with the content. In Hessen, Germany, an official of the Office for Teacher Education noted that teachers trained in the use of mediation with students did not put it into practice due to a lack of confidence with the new skill (Ohio Commission on Dispute Resolution and Conflict Management, 2013). Where it exists, lack of teacher efficacy with peace-focused education highlights the great need for practice with skills. While teacher education programs are responsible for preparing new educators for this practice, certified teachers depend on educational organizations that are available to them for training. Table 2.4 lists some examples of professional organizations in the USA that provide training and guidelines for various aspects of peace-focused education.

Beyond those in war zones, the lack of widely available peace-focused recommendations as government policy results in other organizations recommending a linkage between existing policy and recommended practice (Collaborative for Academic, Social and Emotional Learning, 2015). One response to the dearth of government provision of missing standards is the formation of contextually appropriate ones by cultural interest groups (National Association for Multicultural Education, 2001). For example, the Alaska Standards for Culturally Responsive Schools provide contextually appropriate guidelines for educators of their indigenous populations. Those standards include the following: "Culturally-responsive educators use the local environment and community resources on a regular basis to link what

TABLE 2.4 *Educational organizations in the US providing recommendations*

Organization	Website (2013)
Anti-Defamation League	http://www.adl.org
Teachers Without Borders	http://www.teacherswithoutborders.org
Human Rights Education Association	http://www.hrea.org
National Association for Multicultural Education	http://nameorg.org
North American Association for Environmental Education	www.naaee.net/
Collaborative for Academic, Social, and Emotional Learning	http://casel.org

they are teaching to the everyday lives of the students" (Assembly of Alaska Native Educators, 1998, p. 10). Following is an example of that standard's use. "Educators who meet this cultural standard utilize traditional settings such as camps as learning environments for transmitting both cultural and academic knowledge and skills" (Assembly of Alaska Native Educators, 1998, p. 10). The "traditional setting" of camps, referred to earlier, are seasonal events with their community members where students learn to use their natural resources for skill development in production of food, clothing, tools, and the arts. Learning to fulfill needs with the natural resources of their environment is an aspect of peace-building through sustainability (Earth and Peace Education Associates, 2013; Verhagen, 2004).

Interdependence

Sustainability instruction has been occurring in traditional indigenous education that holds a biocentric worldview. It sees life on planet Earth as interdependent. In this perspective, the task of humans is managing their lives within a web of biological and spiritual interdependence. Hence, damage done to humans and other life forms affects planetary well-being, all forms of life. Concerns about the fact that humans have ventured beyond their planet into their solar system is evident in the policy recommendations of organizations that focus on that issue (such as those of the Global Network Against Weapons and Nuclear Power in Space, 2013; Keating, 2013; Women's International League for Peace and Freedom, 2013). Learning engagement with that issue would cultivate student's cognitive complexity through culturally responsive instruction that allows them to incorporate their norms of thinking and cultural values in peace-focused lessons. By incorporating multiple perspectives of the ways humans interact in and otherwise plan to use outer space, students can enrich their collective evaluation of human engagement with that environment. Ultimately, educational standards that recommend student analysis of contextual conditions of life now and in the future, whether or not the standards are peace focused, can provide rationale for student learning about sustainability in all regions. However, peace-focused standards provide the missing goal in other standards that lack a visionary purpose for analysis of human interactions with their environments and each other.

Standards for peace education

A look at the standards and guidelines designed as recommendations for peace education reveals the types of visions their designers had. The standards listed in the Appendix have three strands of learning: knowledge, skills, and dispositions (Carter, 2013). Due to learning some content of the standards as information and then developing it as a skill, some of the constructs are in multiple strands. For example, self-awareness is knowledge that helps in self-management when facing conflict. With self-awareness, a student can identify a possibility for self-improvement, such as self-control when feeling angry. With awareness of what stimulates their emotions, students use skills of self-management and develop nondestructive outlets for negative feelings.

Standards within each strand are also highly related. Knowledge of pro-active communication supports awareness of how self-management can occur. Contextual awareness includes knowledge of multicultural variations and the common necessities that people of different groups have, including a peaceful environment for fulfillment of their life-sustaining needs. For example, students learn how peacemakers in many cultures shared and acted on common visions of what constitutes a life well lived, interacting with others as you want to be treated. Table 2.5 shows peace education standards for instructional planning.

Clear in this lesson was the application of the disposition empathy, which is a crucial developmental goal during childhood because it is more challenging to inculcate later in life. The lesson plan avoided redundancy in listing empathy as a disposition to be learned. Nevertheless, it included the need to exhibit that attitude in the skill of expressed concern for others. The repetition of concepts across the three strands of the student standards enables teacher connection with them in multiple ways during instructional planning. This freedom to develop lessons with different combinations of cross-referenced standards, or even sole use of one, has been valuable to teachers who design culturally responsive instruction for their students.

The peace education standards for teachers were born from a vision. They support a picture of peace-focused social education by teachers who are responsive to the contexts in which their students live, the cultures their students represent, as well as a vision of a peaceful society. Part of that vision maintains a goal of ensuring learning opportunities

TABLE 2.5 *Instructional planning with related standards*

Lesson Plan
Conflict Analysis and Management
Lesson Rationale   Students need understanding of how speaking with gestures, facial expressions, speech, and writing influence their cognitive and social processes. They need awareness of how communication affects their daily lives and other people.
Peace Education Standards   **Knowledge**   *Pro-active Communication*   Evidence: Identify positively transformation communication techniques   *Methods of Nonviolent Conflict Resolution*   Evidence: Describe appropriate methods for different situations   *Conflict Style*   Evidence: Identify own conflict-response style and alternative methods for resolving disputes   **Skills**   *Analysis of Communication*   Evidence: Identify techniques including representation, bias, balance, multiple perspectives, and active listening   *Empathy*   Evidence: Show understanding of and concern for the suffering of others, whether it was caused by oneself or someone in one's identity group   *Collective and Individual Responsibility*   Evidence: Acknowledge and explain own group or self-contribution to conflict   *Positive Recognition*   Evidence: Acknowledge all efforts and accomplishments of disputants in a conflict

for all students while another part aims at fostering and supporting interactions that maintain and develop peace. Both parts of the vision are significantly interdependent. Peace is an outcome of equity. During inequitable and socially unjust education, useful time spent for instruction is wasted on domination of children whose academic and social needs go unmet (McLaren, 2003). Providing educational opportunities for all students in all subjects, including social interaction, is efficient as well as just (Oakes & Lipton, 1999; Sapon-Shevin, 2010). Learning opportunities increase when students know how to effectively address conflict in constructive ways (Wade, 2007). One of the supports for such accomplishments is Teacher Standard Number 8 (see Appendix) that recommends the creation of a safe place at school for student communication about the violence they perceive and experience. After students obtain relief from the burden of violence, they are less distracted in their lessons. There is less disruption by their behavioral responses to unaddressed needs they have. Teacher Standard Number 9 (see Appendix) encourages the collaboration with students' families in transforming conflict and violence that the students face. In this way, a community of concerned adults works together as co-educators in a school that focuses on peace development. Teacher educators provide experiences for their teacher candidates that cultivate capabilities to effectively work with visions of peace, especially in contexts of direct violence.

In addition to recognizing sources of conflict and violence, teachers-in-training practice the skills for which they will be providing instruction. Therefore, teacher educators facilitate experiential learning opportunities for their students that will build their confidence as well as their knowledge and skills. Supporting the development of teachers who feel prepared for implementation of peace-focused education are standards for teacher educators. Core to those standards are broad contents that enable practice with teaching about controversial issues. Teacher educators facilitate discourse and analytical processes that help students expand their cognitive processes as well as their interaction skills while responding to issues that are included in the curriculum. Teacher Educator Standard 16 (see Appendix) recommends examples and modeling of the skills students need. The Standards for School Administrators (see Appendix) also recommend modeling of dispositions and skills that develop peace.

The different sets of standards are interdependent. Consequently, the administrators share responsibility with the teachers in maintaining an educational program and school milieu that support peace-focused education in both formal as well as informal instruction. The collaborative culture of the school that makes possible such learning results from school-wide commitment with a shared vision. Explicit school mission statements and preparation of all school participants have contributed to the development of such school cultures.

Conclusion

Policy that clearly responds to visions of peace through education has been valuable in the initiation of pedagogy and school practices, which were responsive to students' needs as well as to conflicts in their community. Organizations have resources for development of peace-oriented policy. Foremost in the development of policy is the articulation of visions of a peace in outer space as well as on planet Earth. Additionally important is identification of educational practices that foster shared ideals. Research on peace education supports creation of policy and programs for contextually responsive learning and social cohesion. As cross-cultural contact and cohabitation increases in our world, we can benefit from looking at how different populations responded to strategies designed for advancing peace in their schools and communities. Look about now to see what is working for whom at your school. How might existing peace be built? What type of policy might support that process?

Instruction opportunities

Plan for student review of all of the Standards for Peace Education. Facilitate their critical analysis of the standards and suggestions for revision or expansion of those guidelines to address evident or expected needs. Invite student illustrations, in words or art, of how the standards might be met in a school. For stimulation of campus awareness, arrange for display of those illustrations. Identify current methods of student input on local, state, national, and international policy. Incorporate such input during their response to issues and their planning for the future.

Curricular applications

1. Use the learning cycle for planning a three-phase lesson that enables exploration, development, and expansion of students' peace notions. Incorporate literature and media that expose the students to others' ideas of peace.
2. Plan use in school of greetings and care expressions in many languages. Incorporate heritage norms from students' backgrounds and traditions of others in the local community. Use online resources and communication with students' families for identification and learning about those heritage norms. Have students explain when they might code-switch to communicate with use of traditional or contemporary norms.
3. Review the United Nations Convention on the Rights of the Child (United Nations, 1989). Identify curriculum resources for age-appropriate instruction of your students about the rights that adults envisioned for all children. Ask the students to analyze the

rights and suggest any changes to them they think would help all children have a peaceful present and future.
4   Use the standard in Table 2.3 for Decision Making that incorporates the topic of nonviolent conflict resolution. Plan student identification of situations where people can avoid violence while coping with a difficult conflict.
5   Gather information about indigenous ideas and practices that have contributed to sustainability. Include that information in lessons of different subject areas. Invite a local person of indigenous heritage to school for collaborative teaching. Also plan a trip for students to a site where they can see a demonstration of past or current sustainability.
6   Review the Alaska Standards for Culturally Responsive Schools and find out how they resonate with the educational goals of people in your region. Design instruction for use of cross-generational learning and other aspects of the standards provided by Alaska Native Educators.

Resources for visionary learning

On the Internet

A Guide to Tweeting for Peace and Social Change (http://www.internationalpeaceandconflict.org/profiles/blogs/a-guide-to-tweeting-for-peace-and-social-change#.Uf7g7lPk-Uc)

Gender Guidelines: Peace-Building (http://dmeforpeace.org/sites/default/files/gender_peacebuilding.pdf)

Omniglot, the Language Encyclopedia (http://www.omniglot.com/language/phrases/hello.htm)

UNESCO Culture of Peace, Guidelines for Youth Facilitators, Educators and Teachers (http://en.unesco.org/cultureofpeace/index.php?q=ressources)

UNICEF Convention on the Rights of the Child (www.unicef.org/crc/)

Literature

Wheeler, G., & Vavrus, J. (2009). *Washington state k-12 integrated environmental and sustainability education learning standards.* Olympia, WA: Office of State Superintendent of Instruction. Available at www.k12.wa.us/EnvironmentSustainablity.

Glossary

Dominant culture: the group in a society that has more power than other groups and whose norms are considered "normal."

Galactic community: the known and unknown composition of the galaxy in which people live and their treatment of it.

Standards of complexity: standards that allow accommodation and use of the contextual conditions.

Sustainability: maintaining an ecological balance to sustain the well-being of the natural world and its inhabitants.

Expansion

1 Identify standards from governments and professional societies that recommend aspects of peace education. Check in each subject area of the level in which you provide instruction. Collect those standards in one document you may use for curricular planning.
2 Create a plan for implementing the peace education standards for students. Identify in which subject areas and school activities students could best experience the standards.
3 Create a plan for use of the teacher standards for peace education. Design a self-observational checklist for facilitation of reflection on instructional practices.
4 Write a vision and a mission statement for a school that shows the goal of learning about peace development.
5 Develop a set of peace-focused agreements that could be used as policy in a school. Attend to complexity and cultural norms in the formation of the agreements.
6 Prepare a history of peace policies you can provide to your local government representative in advocacy of peace policy for your region. Describe your vision of peaceful lives there.

3
Responsive Curriculum and Instruction

Abstract: *A broad vision of prosocial education includes informal learning situations along with formal lessons. Purposeful instruction across learning sites mitigates the problem of insufficient attention to social education in schools for children. Responsive curriculum modifications align with instructional recommendations and the cultures in the school's community as well as inclusion of under-represented peoples. The theory of instrumentalism and need for curriculum relevance also justify curriculum adaptation. Responsive instruction perceives and prepares the affective, cognitive, and practical domains of learning. Demonstrations of caring in multiple learning situations, concrete experience, and praxis through vision enactment are essential aspects of responsive peace education.*

Carter, Candice C. *Social Education for Peace: Foundations, Teaching, and Curriculum for Visionary Learning.* New York: Palgrave Macmillan, 2015.
DOI: 10.1057/9781137534057.0007.

A vision of prosocial education is broad, and it includes informal learning situations along with formal ones. This chapter illustrates places and ways in which social education occurs. It paints domains of learning with distinct hues for emphasis on the diversity of teaching opportunities. Instruction occurs across sites of human interaction as well as in subject-focused lessons. Consequently, there are numerous opportunities in schools and their communities for accomplishing peace-oriented learning goals. This situation mitigates the current problem of insufficient attention to social education in the primary and elementary levels of education (Camicia & Saavedra, 2009; Crocco, 1998). It is an outcome of accountability measures involving government testing to check pupils' skills in subjects other than social education. Without accountability for learning outcomes in social education, where states require test-based evidence of student achievement, there has been less instructional time provided in that subject (Misco, Patterson & Doppen, 2011). That curtailing circumstance requires identification and use of the multiple domains in which social education can take place (Schocker et al., 2012; Vogler, 2003). Regardless of the current de-emphasis of social education in regions that do not use standardized tests to assess students' social knowledge, skills, and dispositions, multi-dimensional learning has been worthwhile (Diem, 1996; Merryfield & Remy, 1995; Ndura-Quédraogo & Amster, 2009). Including the same concepts and skills across school situations and activities as well as in subject areas enhances the meaningfulness of those learning contents (Cannon, 2011). Instruction can be responsive to students' needs during informal interactions throughout school as well as in the formal lessons delivered during class time.

Formal curriculum

Formal instruction and informal learning occur with corresponding curricula that incorporate students' affective, cognitive, and practical experiences. All of these domains need consideration when planning instruction. Consequently, this chapter presents them as opportunities for facilitation of learning. The contents of purposeful lessons comprise formal, or explicit, curriculum. Educators and publishers deliberately construct the formal curriculum. It is an outcome of instructional goals and development of means for accomplishing them. In social education, it tends to be oriented toward knowledge and skill development from interaction with literature and media. The creators of the learning materials schools use as curriculum have a strong influence on what the lessons include. Purchased products have become common as curriculum. Standards and guidelines for social education determine how teachers use those products.

Although the stated goals of social education vary across regions, which comparison of standards and guidelines for instruction shows, the curricula are relatively uniform. For example, the state of California includes explicit "literacies" in social education, such as ethical literacy and socio-political literacy (California Department of Education, 1996). Other states do not specify ethics as a major goal and reference point for assessment of student learning. Yet others recommend ethical considerations such as the following from Alaska:

> Culturally-knowledgeable students demonstrate an awareness and appreciation of the relationships and processes of interaction of all elements in the world around them.
>
> Students who meet this cultural standard are able to recognize and build upon the inter-relationships that exist among the spiritual, natural and human realms in the world around them, as reflected in their own cultural traditions and beliefs as well as those of others. (Alaska Native Knowledge Network, 1998, p. 8)

The National Council for the Social Studies (2012) does not specify ethics in its curriculum standards, but it does suggest that students "develop skills in addressing and evaluating critical issues such as peace, conflict, poverty, disease, human rights, trade and global ecology." Meanwhile, the curriculum that schools typically purchase for instruction in social education is rather consistent. Major publishers of textbooks for use in social education typically present the same reified knowledge and skills, regardless of variations in local standards for education and student populations. As such, the contents of the formal curriculum are explicit. They are clearly identifiable and normalizing. In other words, their presentations convey what is "normal" information and ways of thinking about it. The normal information classically presents information about and norms of the dominant culture, with partial information, if any, about those dominated. Color blindness in the standard curriculum of social education has been a continual problem that prevents students from seeing the source of conflicts in their society (Chandler & McKnight, 2009). Social responses to racial characteristics and the role that problem has had in history needs to be a major component of peace-oriented social education. In response to this need, Syd Golston (2010, p. 216) recommends use of a Massachusetts History and Social Science standard along with the standards of the National Council for the Social Studies to promote student answers to questions about overcoming domination: Have we made more progress today in racial equality or equality of the sexes? Are people around the world oppressed more by race or by sex? A vision of equality can help students evaluate progress toward that goal. While some teachers present merely the regularly supplied texts and media for student learning in social education, others modify the formal curriculum.

Curriculum adaptations

Modification of the formal curriculum has several purposes. First, curriculum adaptation occurs for alignment with instructional recommendations. Recommendations in standards for teaching and learning influence what social educators assemble as the formal curriculum. Another purpose is facilitation of learning and development theories that specify what students should have access to as formal curriculum. For example, a theory of peace education clarifies that the format of instruction as well as the content of lessons constitute the curriculum (Galtung & Udayakumar, 2013). Theories of how to provide citizenship education recommend curriculum revision (Thornton, 2004). This selection factor relates closely to another, which is the cultural alignment with the community of the school and the composition of each class, such as those overlooked or underrepresented ethnicities in the supplied curriculum.

With the goal of preparing students for problem solving in a world characterized by diversity, Banks identified four ways of modifying the formal curriculum. This second goal of curriculum modification is inclusion of underrepresented people of the society and nation. The vision Banks has of inclusive curriculum presents not only information about everyone; it pictures students in proactive responses to current conflicts. Table 3.1 lists four revision approaches, with the last one in the list as the most modified curriculum. The major goal of these modes of enhancing students' diversity KSDs is to empower them "to help transform our world and enhance the possibility of human survival" (Banks, 1997).

The facilitation of community-based learning that operationalizes the theory of instrumentalism is the third purpose of curriculum modification. John Dewey emphasized the theory of instrumentalism. Schools

TABLE 3.1 Modes of curriculum modification for diversity knowledge and response

Contributions	Include diverse content as an appendage to the existing curriculum. The added content is typically ethnic heroes and significant events that have been left out of the supplied curriculum
Additive	Add diverse content, throughout the course, without restructuring the existing curriculum
Transformation	Change the curriculum to fully develop diverse content and frameworks for understanding it thereby incorporating the complexity of events and perceptions of them
Social Action	This builds into the transformed curriculum opportunities for students' responses to issues they have analyzed

are instrumental in the facilitation of student involvement in their society (Rugg, 1939). Students need to develop thinking and other skills that help them manage and solve problems (Eldridge, 1998). When students identify an existing problem their community has, acquire information about it, and form reasoned ways of responding to the problem, their education is instrumental. With the theory of instrumentalism and its application in community-based learning, teachers and students encounter conflicts and respond to them. The ideals of the community members as well as the students influence the perceptions of and responses to those conflicts (Marshall, 2011). For example, students can discern the pursuit of corporate success in conflict with the ideals of the community's members that the profit-focused quest does not support. When that pursuit threatens the well-being of several community members, students can identify a structural conflict. Wayne Au reflects in *Teaching about the WTO (World Trade Organization) and Global Issues* (2000) that an instructional outcome was the ability of his students to recognize and understand labor issues in the global community that affected their local neighborhoods. Comprehension of and proactive response to structural conflict can be challenging for students. Yet, its presence in their community provides opportunities for making social studies curriculum highly relevant to their lives.

A fourth factor that influences modification of the formal curriculum is relevance. Violence is a relevant topic in the record of human interactions. Students discover that historical human responses to conflict have been violent and people have the potential to continue or repeat such harm. In multiple ways, students learn about real violence, including horrific events that humans experienced. Memorials, the arts, and literature as well as community conversations about first-hand experiences with societal and global tragedies expose even sheltered children to information about real violence. While some teachers encounter such topics when they arise in students' questions, other educators prepare the contents for student learning. Guidelines for teaching about horrific events are available to educators (Pang, Fernekes & Nelson, 2010; Totten, 1997; Waterson & Haas, 2011). It is important that they take into account the developmental characteristics of the students, including their readiness to comprehend and cope with the realities of human violence.

One major consideration in the analysis and modification of formal curriculum is how the contents may influence social conceptions and dispositions. Students use critical thinking in their analysis of the ways a curriculum features information. Coupled with an ethos of social equity and justice, they can identify undesirable effects that a curriculum's presentation may have. For example, how are the actors in historical events portrayed: as initiators, or passive participants in change? When certain groups such as females, cultural minorities, and youth are not included in the description of an event where they participated, or their activities in change efforts are not mentioned, students miss opportunities to recognize and think about the roles of those participants. This is especially important for students whose conceptions did not characterize those people with high regard before they experienced the curriculum. While those thinking skills are important for student development of critical literacy, it is the responsibility of educators to analyze the curriculum they are selecting or required to use for the multiple ways it presents information (Shor, 2007). Linda Grant De Pauw recognized the need to provide gender inclusion in the story of the American Revolution. Her book *Founding Mothers: Women of America in the Revolutionary Era* (1975) provides snapshots of the daily lives of these women, how they changed during that time period, and their experiences during the Revolution. For example, nurturing by the women and girls was crucial in sustaining the American troops. It also protected the females from the widespread rapes that were being committed by the British army when the females were alone at their homes. "In an age when infection and disease killed far more soldiers than enemy bullets, the traditional women's work—feeding the men, nursing them and keeping them clean—was not expendable to an army" (p. 184). The half-rations for women and quarter rations for children who assisted the American Army during the Revolution had to sustain those volunteers during their efforts to support General Washington's troops and protect themselves from the British.

With the goal of incorporating diverse topics, sources of information, multiple perspectives, critical thinking, and praxis by students, educators balance or replace the provided curriculum with other resources (Berdan et al., 2006; Brophy, 1990). The use of checklists for curriculum contents can help teachers and curriculum designers keep the lessons aligned with their instructional goals. For instance, the "Guidelines for Teaching about American Indian History" that Jack Weatherford (1997) provided has a list of questions to aid critical examination of curriculum resources. One question in that list asks, "Do Indians initiate actions based on their own values and judgments, rather than react to outside factors?" (p. 32). This question highlights the importance of teaching about the beliefs and values of a group that affected their decisions, whether it is in the presentation of history or just literature about their ways of living. At the core of all groups are conceptions of the future and values that determine right behaviors in the culture. Helping students identify and analyze these common components of cultures can enable their recognition of intergroup similarities. They can see that displaying particular behaviors are valued in all groups, and achievement of the groups' goals as a society is dependent on those behaviors. Hence, each society has a way of teaching those behaviors. For example, each cultural group and society has a manner of showing respect. Curriculum that shows how people in different cultures convey respect along with information about the beliefs that underlie their actions has multiple purposes. It stimulates affective responses to the different norms people have, cognitive processes for understanding those behaviors, and practical value in learning them for use in multicultural interactions.

When the formal curriculum includes examples of anti-social behaviors, analysis of its presentation as well as human interactions in the face of conflict can take place. Violent images as well as descriptions of violent situations include techniques that affect perception of the subject matter. Curriculum resources that explain those techniques are instructive. For instance, the collection of propaganda images that Sam Keen assembled, titled *Faces of the Enemy* (1986) has a poem that describes ways to stimulate enmity. An anti-social feeling toward the subject, such as hostility, results from enmity. Lines from Keen's poem describe the process of hiding the diversity of humanity's individual characteristics. "Obscure the sweet individuality of each face. Erase all hints of the myriad loves, hopes, fears that play through the kaleidoscope of every finite heart" (p. 9). Analysis of informal as well as formal curriculum can aid in the identification of how particular words and illustrations determine conceptions and orientations to peace.

Implicit curriculum

The implicit, also called the informal, curriculum provides an abundance of contexts for student learning. All of the interactions that occur in an educational setting comprise the implicit curriculum. It occurs as situated learning (Goel et al., 2010). Hence, students continually absorb and process information from their experiences. Intentional planning of students' activities throughout the school enhances the implicit curriculum. Places in the school where students interact with others are rich contexts for expanding as well as assimilating conceptions of peace. Those situations exist in visual displays, the language usage, and nonverbal communication of staff, teachers, and administrators, along with the handling of materials in the school.

The environment

The physical environment of the school has several spaces where educators can promote peace through an ethos of care in the class and school. When students of high school teacher Mary Maio (2007) were asked to illustrate peace, they predominately identified interpersonal relationships that were supportive, especially in situations of conflict. Their projects to make brief videos as public service announcements which depicted peace happening often featured conflict situations with school members and how those could be quickly resolved. Their scenarios demonstrated use of the senses to discern needs and creativity for addressing them. For example, in noticing a student sitting alone in the lunch area, peace was providing personal company for the student. It was just one of many expressions of empathy their brief award-winning videos expressed. Illustrations by students of the places in schools and their community where peace could occur can uncover for educators several spaces for explicit instruction and support for peace development.

Once students and other members of the school identify contexts for advancing peace, analysis of the interactions in those spaces is the next step in planning the implicit curriculum of peace advancement. In her ongoing analysis and explanation of school contexts that present multiple forms of structural and relational conflicts for students, bell hooks (2003) emphasizes the importance of building community across the many divisions societies and their schools perpetuate in the implicit curriculum. While reminding educators of how oppression occurs in such situations, she promotes in her chapter "Heart to Heart" the expression of care for and love of students. Others have also described the importance of showing sincere concern for students and listening to them (Lin, 2006; Miller, 2006; Rosenberg, 2003). While providing the implicit curriculum through modeling, educators "must create small corners of loving consideration and live peace" (Hoffman, 2008, p. 22).

Compassionate communication demonstrates empathetic discourse that supports identification of needs. Active listening shows students respect and concern while modeling a problem-solving process (Hart, S., 2004). There are free resources for learning the techniques of compassionate communication. The New Conversations Initiative (2015) is an open-source library with guides that educators and families of the students can access free. The Center for Nonviolent Communication (2013) offers several books for educators and others, for learning applications of this technique in many different situations. Free resources on the center's website include a model for nonviolent communication and vocabulary lists to help with clarification of feelings and needs in association with a conflict.

Vocabulary curriculum

Identification of needs in a conflict is more challenging when people lack a broad vocabulary for expressing their feelings. Replying with the word "bad" in response to a question about feeling renders the need less apparent than use of a more informative descriptor, such as "ignored," "left out," or "cheated." School staff can help teach students how to clarify their feelings in conflict by asking questions that prompt learning of the needed vocabulary: "Are you feeling cheated? If not, what do you feel now when you think about the problem?" A seed in the feeling descriptor has roots in the problem. Feeling cheated can indicate a perception of injustice. Once clarified, the next step of solving the problem can begin. Practice with these modes of compassionate communication by students in theatrical performances has been an entertaining way to help them learn the needed techniques of peace-oriented interaction. For example, students in San Benito High School used participation theater in school assemblies to practice the techniques of active listening in problem-based skits (Lovejoy, 2007). Student members of the audience volunteered to replace the protagonist with an antagonist in each skit for solving a conflict. The means used were compassionate communication and creativity. The audience expressed enjoyment watching their peers use impromptu acting while working through typical conflicts the teenagers experienced in their lives. Such techniques are also useful for revisiting historical events and changing what happened to render solutions without violence. Whether as formal or informal curriculum, the theatrical activities of students are ripe for expressing visions of a better life and world. Participation theater offers them a way to change the behaviors of characters and the outcome of the conflicts they are facing (Korty, 2002). An aspect of behavioral change is careful selection of words in any communication, especially conflict situations.

Monitoring the vocabulary as well as tone of words stated by school members around the campus could foster promotion of peace. They can answer the question, "Are you a humanizer?" that Gomes de Matos (2002) recommended for helping school employees and students check their sense of self-respect along with respect for others. The Hague Appeal for Peace (2013) provides a free lesson for educators that has eight checkpoints for identifying "I am a humanizer when I..." Educators can carefully select their vocabulary to avoid expressions of violence that have become commonplace. For example, one can rephrase the statement of killing two birds with one stone to feeding two birds with one scone. Analysis of language usage for offensive and violent expressions starts with internal thoughts and then progresses to external expressions.

Awareness of self-talk, or internal thought, is crucial to conversion of interpersonal exchanges and even the success of physical accomplishments. Strategies that have been helpful for students and athletes are self-examination and monitoring, along with relaxation skills for coping with stress and positive imagery (Gilbert & Orlick, 1996; Orlick, 2008). In addition to monitoring vocabulary for negativity and violence, critical analysis of it reveals the roots of societal conflicts (Oxford, 2013). For example, gender inclusiveness expressed by terms such as humankind, versus mankind, and students or colleagues versus "guys," demonstrates the vision of balanced representation in society. The emerging field of Peace Linguistics calls to attention the many ways that peace relates to aspects of communication (Friedrich, 2007). Critical analysis of language usage uncovers the roots of social conflicts in school and society. A conflict that has hidden roots indicates an opportunity for transformation.

Hidden curriculum

The hidden curriculum exists throughout the school. The norms, values, and beliefs that the school promotes through the arrangements in the physical facility, the displays there, the interactions of the school members as well as the formal lessons comprise the hidden curriculum. In other words, all of the interactions in the school and the facilitation of them by the employees provide learning contexts. For example, Myles, Trautman, and Schelvan (2004) identify the following aspects of school as sites for analysis and management of learning situations: bathroom rules, eating, clothing, figurative speech and idioms, slang terms, and so on. The ways that the school employees express expectations of particular types of students is another example of the hidden curriculum. For instance, differences of expectations for male versus female behaviors need analysis (Sharp, 2012). Cultural expectations, beyond differentiation of gender, take expression in the approval or discouragement of different social norms. Analysis and purposeful design of the hidden curriculum is crucial for visionary education. That analysis includes identification of hierarchy and privilege, known as cultural capital (Bourdieu & Passeron, 1990). Some students have an advantage at the school due to the alignment of their norms and identities, and their parents' abilities to successfully interact with the school's employees. That advantage is a form of cultural capital (Dumais, 2002). Another facet of it is their representation in the lesson contents, such as greater representation of their gender or ethnicity. They see who are the main subjects of the formal curriculum and leaders in the informal curriculum. In their analysis of secondary education, Konidari and Abernot (2008) found deficits in the hidden curriculum when they examined it: involvement, affiliation, teacher support, order/organization, rule clarity, and task orientation for secondary students. The communication deficit limits intrapersonal and intergroup well-being. The relational deficit evidences a lack of social cohesion that supports positive interdependence in collaborative experiences and shared identities.

Table 3.2 provides questions for school members to use in identification, analysis, and transformation of the hidden curriculum.

Visionary education aims to disrupt the inequalities that the hidden curriculum reproduces. The goal is promotion of equal opportunities for peaceful lives. With the extensiveness of the hidden curriculum, there are many opportunities to revise it.

TABLE 3.2 *Hidden curriculum*

Physical environment	Whose cultures are practiced?
Social interactions	Which norms are promoted and why?
Power relations	Who has the power in different situations?
Transformation	What ways can the power be redistributed for equality?

Transformation of the hidden curriculum involves analysis by school members for the ways it might be improved. Examples of implicit strategies include communication with students and their families, as well as diverse members of the community who act as cultural consultants when the school employees do not represent the student population. Strategies for that communication include direct as well as distant interaction. Those connections are family and community participation in planning and other school functions, visits of school staff with students' families off campus, along with distant interaction through phone calls, e-mails, and surveys. For example, educators conduct a needs-assessment survey of students' families for input on the physical and social arrangements in the school. Teachers do the same with the formal curriculum when they are planning lessons and other activities their students may engage in during class time, such as student involvements in the graphic and performing arts (Duckworth, Allen, & Williams, 2012; Lee, 2013). Incorporating multiple genres of arts helps students cross cultural borders (Saafir, 2012). Gender balance in visual displays made around the school as well as the classrooms communicates the equal importance of females. Instead of featuring the accomplishments in March during Women's History Month, schools can find and make displays to meet the goal of gender balance. The 2013 theme of the National Women's History Project (2013) is Women Inspiring Innovation through Imagination. This brings to mind all of the celebrated, and less known, women whose imaginations were the foundation of needed changes made. There are several ways to find expression of those changes, including lyrics of music.

Musical genres and the messages in the music are rich sources of hidden curriculum. An example is prosocial music played during learning periods, transition, and social times throughout various areas of the school (Carter, 2003). It allows students to absorb messages that foster peace-oriented interactions. The music included in school assemblies and break sites in a school for students and faculty needs examination for inclusivity and lyrical contents. While examining the informal curriculum of holidays the school acknowledges, celebrates, and incorporates in the formal curriculum for cultural inclusivity, there is also a need to avoid the superficial treatment of cultural celebrations. In her chapter "The Establishment of Liberatory Alliances with People of Color," Antonia Darder (2011) points out the need to not strip that content of its deep meanings and often revolutionary intent in the historical period the celebrations recall. School members can start with curriculum resources that include the history of holidays and build on that for inclusion of the needed content where the school presents the holiday (Polon & Cantwell, 1983). Obtaining that information from ethnic groups that celebrate the holiday and sharing it with all families of the students has been a popular inclusion strategy that I have used across primary, secondary, and higher education. Connecting the performing arts with the history of special days in different cultures and teaching about those days thematically, based on their common messages within the cultures that celebrate them, were strategies facilitated with the involvement of community members.

Community involvement

Enlisting community participation and support for revision of the curriculum and instruction is a crucial task for visionary educators. One way to facilitate regular involvement of the community is with the use of Study Circles (Mengual, 2008). In a study circle, participants discuss topics that pertain to an issue or need (Campbell, 1998). A neutral facilitator helps participants, who have varying amounts of cultural capital, with description of needs they perceive. The involvement of diverse members of a community enables awareness-raising and collaborative problem solving. Typically, the circle sessions last many weeks and culminate with a plan by the participants for making changes to address the needs they identified.

Another way community conferencing has occurred is through implementation of restorative practices. In response to conflicts that students experience in the school, a conference for discussion between the participants occurs with the aim of restoring the relationships of those who are directly involved in a conflict. The goal of repairing harm done is also germane to restoration. The schools have restorative practices adapted from indigenous cultures. A whole-school approach to restoration involves voluntary communication by school and community members in the conferences (Hopkins, 2004). With the vision of a healed community, participants talk about feelings, identities, and needs. Caring for everyone, not just the school's well-being, is the goal which some of the recent facilitations of restorative practices have evidenced (Carter, 2012). The hidden curriculum of restorative practices needs analysis in a school to check for its authenticity. This involves the well-being of community members, versus a narrower focus on student compliance and discipline. Looking at the roots of conflicts that discipline problems evidence can reveal structural conflicts the community has that are affecting students' experiences in the schools. Use of the conferences and circles as informal curriculum illustrates the instructional opportunities they present (Pranis, 2005).

Informal instruction

Responsive instruction occurs informally in the contexts mentioned earlier as students observe and interact on their campus. Informal learning starts before students begin their matriculation in schools. Educators carry on from where students are in cognitive, social, and physical development when they arrive at school. Hence, there is much for educators to observe about students during their preparation for responsive lessons. All of those observations are also useful for informal instruction. In other words, being keen listeners and observers of others is an aspect of intercultural development. In a pluralistic society with a goal of peace, the ability to understand, value, and accommodate different ways of knowing and being is important. School members teach these processes informally by modeling (Lieber, 2003). Through demonstrations of respect, compassion, and fairness in school, its members foster ethics and integrity (Mirk, 2013).

Indirect instruction involves showing students skills in communication and cross-cultural participation, along with caring for life forms and their environment. Students observations in their learning environment constitutes "caught" lessons, versus the "taught" ones of formal instruction (Crawford, 2005). Observing Dr. Martin Luther King Jr.'s statement "Peace is not merely a distant goal we seek, but a means by which we arrive at that goal" can be useful to school members for monitoring their social thoughts and interactions (as cited in Crawford, 2005, p. 322).

Thinking aloud by school staff reveals dispositions and cognitive processes that support social understanding and cohesion. This is especially useful for modeling desired responses to conflicts. This is exemplified in the statement, "I wonder if [that person] feels disempowered because s/he is not being selected for..." Through the spoken thought processes, the components of transformation serve as informal instruction. School members can informally teach several aspects of transformation.

TABLE 3.3   *Transformation of knowledge*

Activating event
Articulating assumptions
Openness to alternatives
Discourse
Revision of assumptions and perspectives
Action on revisions

Table 3.3 lists phases that occur in cycles of response to occurrences (Cranton 2002 in Saafir, 2012, p. 265). By speaking about all of these phases in one's thinking, students can discern change that builds upon understanding. In many situations, it is educative to voice curiosity in response to conflicts along with contemplating how to resolve them.

Contemplation, recently infused in Western education, supports envisioning as well as learning about others as a response to conflict (Hart, T., 2004; Hill, Herndon, & Karpinska, 2006). Contemplation transpires through different approaches, including meditation, yoga, guided imagery, and periods of silence in the schools. The Tree of Contemplative Practices that the Center for Contemplative Mind in Society (2013) presents has many branches that illustrate not only methods of contemplation, but also outcomes, including actions to address conflicts. Due to the newness of this activity in secular schools of the USA, students could benefit from seeing it modeled.

Demonstrating peace-oriented dispositions and practices is a powerful form of education that has been the catalyst for subsequent praxis of the observing mentees (Harris, 2013). Demonstrations can include explained choices predicated on values that determine behaviors. Those informal lessons occur in displays of deference to elders, multilingual/multiculturalism, sustainable treatment of materials, food selection, consumption of fairly traded goods, and restoration efforts as well as prevention of injustice and harm. By talking about how these actions have occurred away from campus along with demonstrating them at the school, the informal lessons can augment formal instruction in which students learn how such actions have led to peace.

Formal instruction

Formal instruction occurs in situations wherein students are aware of lessons and evaluation of their learning progress. Responsively, visionary lessons are experiential, culturally diverse, developmentally appropriate, constructive, holistic, community oriented, and prosocial. Peace-promoting lessons incorporate local and global communities with contextually responsive instruction that addresses individual as well as societal needs (Montessori, 1972). The formal instruction accommodates students' individual needs with different ways that enable their accomplishments in social education. There is a cogent recommendation that we "privilege the perspectives of racial, ethnic, poor and transnational students...to benefit both national and transnational students by increasing the range of cultural, global and democratic perspectives in the curriculum" (Camicia & Saavedra, 2009, p. 513).

Design of students' experiences focuses on students' needs and the instructional goals of social education. The task involves purposeful planning for experiences that will connect the individual and cultural traits of the students with the prescribed content and the current realities of it in local to global contexts (Gay, 2000; Morgan & Vandrick, 2009). Avoidance of politics is not part of the planning. With a realization that experience is the foundation of understanding and skill development, teachers enable students to perceive and analyze needs as well as to prepare for and actively respond to them (Totten & Pedersen, 2013). Including social issues in the formal as well as the informal curricula gives students multiple opportunities to think about, discuss, and respond to needs with their orientation toward peace (Evans & Saxe, 1996; Ochoa-Becker, 2007; Totten & Pedersen, 2012). This humanistic pedagogy aims to prevent apathy and promote praxis (Muller, 2012). While there are several approaches to incorporation of social issues in the formal curriculum, inclusion of the student's history and cultures is optimal for the relevance of the contents and student participation in the lessons.

Incorporation of students' cultural norms and those in the surrounding society broadens intercultural competencies including learning, understanding, and acting in different ways. It honors students' backgrounds and the members of the community while it incorporates norms of their families and others who live around them. By facilitating multiple ways of learning and acting, teachers and counselors can help children adapt to the challenges they face, building peace in the present as a foundation for the future (Gernstein & Moescheberger, 2003).

Developmental responsiveness involves planning differentiated learning that allows and enables student participation in a variety of ways (Glass, 2011; Westwood, 2011; Wilson & Papadonis, 2006). It also clarifies assessment criteria and provides fair evaluation of student learning.

TABLE 3.4 *Case example*

The Singing Strike and the Rebel Students Singing

Students who had just finished doing the role play on the Industrial Workers of the World and the 1912 Lawrence, Massachusetts, textiles strike, known as "the singing strike," were allowed to create their own public demonstration in response to a current conflict. In the Literature and US History class of their high school, the students had been learning about democratic action in response to structural conflicts. When they and their teachers felt insulted by a local newspaper's article that rendered a disrespectful description of their diversely populated school and the violence in its community, the students spent their class time organizing their response. It represented the student's stand against irresponsible journalism and the racism they discerned in its roots. As their public action, they sang folk songs while they marched in mass to the headquarters of the newspaper where they sought a dialogue with the writer and editor of the offending article.

One teacher reflected that:

> This sudden outburst of student activism was, in fact, not so sudden. Over the year, Linda's and my class focused on issues of social justice and resistance---ours was a "talk back" curriculum. We wanted students to feel themselves part of an American, even international, tradition of struggle against oppression. (Bill Bigelow, 1993, p. 3)

Informing students of the learning goals and outcomes fairly informs them about evaluation of their learning. When students do not know what the teacher needs to observe as evidence of learning, students are not fairly equipped to demonstrate their learning success. That student awareness is crucial in addition to teacher knowledge of students' norms, individual traits, talents, and motivations that affect their responses to curriculum (Chandler & McKnight, 2012; Epstein, 2001). Learning accommodations are practices and procedures that provide equitable access to lesson contents and display of learning from them. Hence, constructivism is not only a process of student learning, but also a process of lesson and assessment preparation. Partnership with students' families and community members enhances constructive planning for culturally responsive and individualized instruction (Eisler, 2000). Harold Rugg's (1931, p. 288) recommendation for a "school-centered community" included collaboration between local organizations.

Constructing notions of peace includes synthesis of many ideas about how to live and learn without causing harm. Postmodern and liberal notions of peace and how to teach about it demonstrate their shared aspects in the formal curriculum (Ghaderi, 2011). Understanding human similarities amidst cultural and other differences is a common goal of peace-oriented learning. Although they each have a filter of cultural values and norms in the vision of peace, students construct their conceptions of lives without harm in different situations. Their exposure to issues in the natural and social realms presents opportunities to evaluate past and current practices. This includes critical analysis of shared power, resource management, and opportunities for living healthy lives. For teaching this with the prescribed history curriculum, Cannon (2011) acquires a rich collection of resources that students can use for broadening and deepening their knowledge through analysis with multiple sets of information. The critical analysis her students do of the different data precedes their reinvention of historical communities and events. The historical utopia they construct features equality, fairness, and other conditions of peaceful interaction. These utopias Cannon's students reconstruct from situations that were characterized by structural, if not direct, violence, involved literacy, writing, and graphic arts. As mentioned earlier, the performing arts have also been positive elements in the formal curriculum as a means of student learning. By using an aesthetic sign system other than language, students can express their understanding of content and their visions. Sign systems are ways people make and share meaning (Harste, 2000). My colleagues and I have found tableau to be a useful activity for assessment of student's prior knowledge before experiencing the formal curriculum and illustration of their understanding after a lesson or unit (MacPhee & Whitecotton, 2011). A tableau is a scene students create in any space that can be their stage with themselves as silent and motionless actors. Their creation of the scene is a prosocial act and a holistic experience. Students can co-construct the scene from their collective notion of its meaning, and they use multiple aspects of their physical as well as mental selves in its creation. Their expressions of peace events, such as an act of forgiveness by the harmed, are affective for the observers as well as the actors. Affect is an important factor in learning and recall of the curriculum contents. The holistic learning approach and prosocial focus for envisioning peaceful contexts often result with interdisciplinary learning. For example, when students exercised their ecological imaginations to construct and depict better environments for life, "they broadened the scope of their imaginations to consider how these better states of affairs could benefit the environment and the community. This process occurred organically as their ecological solutions often intersected with social, economic and aesthetic ones" (Bertling, 2013, p. 38). Holistic instruction facilitates connections between multiple aspects of being human (Lynn, 2008; Miller, 1990).

Realms of learning

Informal as well as formal instruction involves planning in three realms of learning. Holistic education involves planning for the affective, cognitive, and practical realms of learning. In the affective domain, students' physical and psychological states need consideration. With awareness that those states can help students absorb information, think more clearly, and expand their skills, lesson planning attends to the affect that is likely in a learning situation. For example, how might students feel about a current problem that can be threatening to any of them? Considerations in that planning include the climate of the classroom and other places where students interact (Hester, n.d.). Teachers can ask themselves while planning: *What might be students' levels of physical comfort and psychological well-being? Will controversy and conflicts included in the lessons cause such negative affect that student learning will be hindered? How can student involvement in problem solving be rendered as non-threatening to them and instead be a source of empowerment? What components of transformative learning should be included?*

The affective realm of learning involves the formation and change of attitudes through student observations and experiences, with incorporation of their emotions (Helmsing, 2014; Miller, 2001; Zembylas & McGlynn, 2012). Development and changes occur in a process whereby each student "organizes values into priorities by contrasting different values, resolving conflicts between them, and creating a unique value system. The emphasis is on comparing, relating and synthesizing values" (Clark, 2010, para. 10).

The process of synthesizing values, analyzing how peace has happened throughout human history, and applying skills for peace development involves the three realms of learning. For example, the student disposition of optimism may result from discernment of prosocial values demonstrated in the school by teachers along with their efforts to help students resolve conflicts without harm. Learning in a safe and comfortable milieu about conflict keeps the affective filter low and aids students in the cognitive realm. It also encourages them to try out strategies of conflict management. Building the disposition of courage to do new or different things in a community is an important goal involving the affective, cognitive, and practical aspects of learning (Diamond, 2000).

The cognitive realm of responsive education involves students in the higher (analysis, synthesis, and evaluation) as well as lower (knowledge and comprehension) levels of thinking. Students obtain information and analyze it from different perspectives. "A plurality of social perspectives is a social good" that Parker (2003, p. 108) illustrates in his description of deliberation as social education. It is important to help them recognize dichotomy, which is how the media typically presents conflict in only two frames for analysis. In their pursuit of collecting more information to avoid dichotomous analysis, students can learn triangulation. In that method of identifying at least three different ways of representing a situation, students can discern its complexities and balance representations of it. This cognitive process reveals the relevance of seeking cross-cultural and multiple-perspective information about a conflict. It is practical for need identification in a conflict to get information from everyone involved in it, and outside observers see the situation differently. Each perspective of the conflict may be useful in creating a practical resolution. My own students use this method in analysis of a current social issue that is important to them before they construct and implement a transformational response to it.

Maria Montessori articulated the practical realm of instruction when she recognized the need for education to incorporate the tasks that students must accomplish throughout their current and future lives. This domain of learning has immediacy in that it enables students to recognize the usefulness of their learning experiences. With its importance in their present and envisioned lives, the practical realm occurs through partnership with others in the student's community as well as in their school and class. For example, learning to bear witness to the painful experience of another, without judgment and directives, builds community while relieving suffering. Rachel Kessler (2005) explains an outcome of council circles in the Passageways curriculum she used. "As our students learn to keep their hearts and minds open to both the suffering and joy of their schoolmates, the 'will to do no harm' is awakened or strengthened" (p. 69). By demonstrating the practicality of caring, through silent listening, students experience a demonstration of empathetic morality (Noddings, 2010). Their experiences with each other provide a model for responsiveness as well as a means for understanding, which incorporate affective, cognitive, and practical learning (Table 3.5).

Conclusion

Responsive curriculum and instruction can occur throughout the school to increase the relevancy of social education as well as to accomplish its needed expansion. There are many physical contexts and social situations in which educators can plan, prepare, and facilitate instruction that fosters peace-oriented learning. Relational interactions and the arrangements of the school for them as well as representation of students' backgrounds are the informal curriculum. Preparation of and planning with students' families as co-teachers provides an opportunity to make needed cultural alignments of the formal and informal lessons. In the same vein, partnership with students' families and community members renders a model of regard and interdependence as informal instruction. The demonstration of caring about everyone in a community of learners, the society in which they live, and the natural environment are concrete experiences for building visions of future actions.

Responsive social education fosters learning in multiple ways and for practical purposes, including student actions for an improved society that manages conflict without violence and repairs harm. Educators and their community partners have found several ways for incorporating such learning across disciplines as well as school contexts. This accomplishment shows the relevance of peace-focused learning and its feasibility, even during the current wave of accountability-focused instruction.

TABLE 3.5   *Identification and communication with others connected in conflict*

Lesson Plan

Peace Partners Here and There

Lesson Goal
Students will identify the others in school, their community, and the world who are their Peace Partners in conflict management.

Exploration
Students identify one or more people who are connected to them in systemic conflicts such as economic injustice, natural resource depletion, interethnic avoidance, and so on.

Development
Students show, explain, diagram, or otherwise demonstrate their understanding of the interdependence they have with their Peace Partner. For instance, who is the producer of their shoes and how well does the person who provides its materials and the person who constructs the shoes live with ample resources for a healthy life? Who in their school is connected to them in sustainable use of its resources? Who in the school is disadvantaged by societal response to characteristics such as race, ethnic identity, gender, sexual orientation, or disability?

Expansion
Students write letters, conversations, scripts for plays, and poetry that demonstrate compassionate communication about perceptions of their peace partners, needs in the conflict, and possibilities for proactively resolving the conflict in which they are connected.

Instruction opportunities. Teach students about caught lessons in their surroundings. They can document and analyze messages in visual and physical interactions as well as discourse. Have them reflect on their own identities and experiences that might influence their perceptions of their surroundings and interactions in it. Create a comfortable milieu for continual sharing of their observations. Enable questions, open or anonymous, from others in response to their observations and explanations of the surroundings they observed.

Curricular applications

1. Facilitate student visions of equity on and beyond your campus. Plan informal ways for their identification of inequities they perceive. These might be anonymous statements made by them and collected for analysis and response. They can categorize identified opportunities for greater equality on campus. Invite their suggestions for improving equality on campus and then plan with other campus members changes that would demonstrate pursuit of that goal.
2. Identify a conflict in their community about which students recently expressed concern. Analyze the current curriculum's presentation of the conflict topic in each subject area. Plan improvement of that learning content and facilitation of student response to the conflict.
3. Arrange for student analysis of images around them in any sources that promote enmity. Help them identify the artistic techniques in each image that stimulates negative thoughts and emotions. Enable student communication with producers of current media that can cause anti-social feelings toward an identity group.
4. Describe how the implicit curriculum at your school can be improved to foster peace. What in the physical environment could be changed? What opportunities are there for modeling compassionate communication?
5. When and where on your campus could students engage in participation theater? Explain one or more opportunities for their voluntary involvement in skits or plays that present conflicts in which they can try peace strategies.
6. In a lesson plan for student visioning, describe the affective, cognitive, and practical goals of the instruction. Elaborate how you

will manage the students' physical and psychological experiences. Identify the practical aspects of the learning experience.

Resources for visionary learning

On the Internet

Artists Culture of Peace (http://www.sgi-usa.org/newsandevents/exhibitions/ArtistsAsPeacemakers-Web-Dec07.pdf)
A Guide for Training Study Circle Facilitators (http://www.awcnet.org/documents/tools_studycirclefacilitatorsguide.pdf)
The National Women's History Project (http://www.nwhp.org/)
The New Conversations Initiative (http://www.newconversations.net/)
Richmond Peace Education Center (http://www.rpec.org/)
Urban Improv (http://www.urbanimprov.org/)

Literature

Bartkowski, M. J. (ed.). (2013). *Recovering nonviolent history: Civil resistance in liberation struggles.* London: Lynne Rienner.
Boulding, E. 2000. *Cultures of peace: The hidden side of history.* Syracuse, NY: Syracuse University.
De Pauw, L. G. (1975). *Founding mothers. Women of America in the Revolutionary Era.* Boston: Houghton Mifflin.
Hague Appeal for Peace. (2013). Are you a humanizer? Retrieved from http://www.haguepeace.org/files/morePeaceLessons/Are%20You%20A%20Humanizer%20(Francesco%20Brazil).pdf
Keen, S. (1986). *Faces of the enemy. Reflections of the hostile imagination.* New York, NY: Harper and Row.
New York Collective of Radical Educators. (2013). *Planning to change the world: A plan book for social justice teachers 2013–1014.* Milwaukee, WI: Rethinking Schools. Available from http://www.rethinkingschools.org/
Saldaña, J. (1995). *Drama of color. Improvisation with multiethnic folklore.* Portsmouth, NH: Heinemann.
Silverman, J. (1992). *Songs of protest and civil rights.* New York: Chelsea House.
Warren, W. (1999). *Black women scientists in the United States.* Bloomington, IN: Indiana University.

Wilhelm, J. D., & Edmiston, B. (1998). *Imagining to learn. Inquiry, ethics, and integration through drama.* Portsmouth, NH: Heinemann.

Glossary

Critical literacy: analysis of the text's presentation of information for perspective, descriptors, omitted content, and other conceptual factors.

Hidden curriculum: the informal learning content that shapes perceptions and often differentiates power between populations.

Cultural capital: the traits and norms that are valued in a society, which provide greater chances of success and privilege.

Instrumentalism: inclusion of societal problems in the curriculum and student learning through interaction with them.

Praxis: deliberate response to conflict that involves actions for making needed changes. It is an outcome of analytic thinking in formation of the conflict response.

Reify: maintain a concept or status through its perpetuation in the curriculum.

Expansion

1 Explain how the formal social studies curriculum is relevant to your students' lives. Describe the diversity of your school's student population and their cultural representation in the formal curriculum. How could you improve the formal curriculum for those who are not represented in it?
2 Describe the physical and social contexts that comprise the hidden curriculum at your school. What messages about power does that curriculum convey? How might one revise the curriculum to promote power equity?
3 Describe how formal instruction at your school could become more prosocial and holistic. How could a partnership approach to education improve formal instruction in social education there? What might students' families and community members do to foster students' visions of a peaceful future?

4 Write a true or imaginary story about a teacher who used these components of peace-oriented social education: modeling, thinking aloud, description of thinking, and corresponding experiences beyond the school.
5 Identify practical-life experiences on and off campus for student use of social analysis and interaction skills. How might they expand cross-cultural communication to discern several perspectives of a conflict in their local and global communities?
6 Facilitate a Council Circle in your class or in a community where participants describe their feelings about a current structural or intrapersonal conflict. Practice compassionate expressions of empathy through body language without making judgmental comments. Have participants illustrate and discuss their visions of life without those conflicts.

4
Transdisciplinary and Powerful Learning

Abstract: *Powerful social studies for peace engages students in all aspects of life. Transdiciplinarity combines different forms of knowledge through inquiry across disciplines and cultures. It is distinct from interdisciplinary and multidisciplinary work in that it enables new areas of specialization, like peace studies, gender studies and multicultural education. The National Council for the Social Studies in the USA described powerful teaching and learning as outcomes of: integrative, meaningful, value-based, challenging, and active instruction. Visioning about the near and far future enhances powerful social studies by orienting students toward a future without harm as a response to conflict.*

Carter, Candice C. *Social Education for Peace: Foundations, Teaching, and Curriculum for Visionary Learning.* New York: Palgrave Macmillan, 2015.
DOI: 10.1057/9781137534057.0008.

Visionary education involves transdisciplinary learning. Pursuing peace engages students in powerful social studies involving all aspects of life. In addition to the disciplines that social education has included, people also need for conflict management the knowledge base and skill sets in other disciplines.

Transdisciplinarity combines different forms of knowledge through inquiry across disciplines and cultures (Nicolescu, 2002). Scientific methods of inquiry established in modern times comprise one component of transdisciplinarity. Another component incorporates observations that respond to the findings, which is an inclusive manner of discovery and synthesis (Mobjörk, 2010). In other words, feedback on perceptions of conclusions made from inquiry is a component of the analytical process. Considered in transdisciplinary learning are the insights of others not situated within the study and field. In an effort to avoid hegemonic and unidirectional approaches that limit knowledge advancement, the process involves reintegration of ancient and indigenous forms of information with multiple ways of understanding it. This process avoids the limitations that methods of "modern" science have had (Somerville & Rapport, 2000; Nabudere, 2012). Use of the multi-systems toolbox for working with human thinking responds to a polarized and otherwise limited worldview that constrains problem solving. The division of knowledge bases into disciplines facilitates specializations that limit the tools of discovery and problem solving when they are not all available together (Somerville & Rapport, 2000).

The need to cross disciplinary boundaries in social education has been evident in the subject area of social studies. Its inclusion of multiple disciplines demonstrates more than the integrative nature of social education. It illuminates the synergy that teachers need for accomplishing the goal of providing integrative instruction (Levin & Nevo, 2009; Richards, 2012). Transdisciplinarity is distinct from interdisciplinary and multidisciplinary work in that it enables new areas of specialization, such as conflict resolution (Carter, 2010a). Multidisciplinary work allows many specializations to investigate the same problem, and methods of those inquiries, such as qualitative inquiry transferred across disciplines in an interdisciplinary manner. In this way, transdisciplinarity features new fields of learning, including peace studies (Lappin, 2009). The development of transdisciplinary curriculum requires integration. It is one of several components with which educators construct powerful social education.

The National Council for the Social Studies in the USA produced a position statement that described powerful teaching and learning as outcomes of integrative, meaningful, value-based, challenging, and active instruction. Each of those pedagogical techniques have been incorporated for instruction through

> strategies and activities that engage students with significant ideas, and encourages them to connect what they are learning to their prior knowledge and to current issues, to think crucially and creatively about what they are learning, and to apply that learning to authentic situations. (National Council for the Social Studies, 2008, para. 5)

The components of powerful social education needs elaboration in preparation for use of that transformation-oriented pedagogy.

Integrated and holistic development

Integration of curriculum and instruction has been done in several ways while waxing and waning as a learning method during the past century. For instance, Fogarty and Stoehr (1991) identified ten classifications of curriculum integration including: fragmented, nested, shared, threaded, immersed, connected, sequenced, webbed, and networked. Although integration has been advocated, challenges exist in its rationale and facilitation (Alleman & Brophy, 1991). The curriculum design for integrated learning has had constraints from demands for standards-based and test-oriented instruction, along with inconclusive evidence for the effects of implementing integrated curriculum. The multiple ways curriculum integration has been designed and facilitated have impeded generalization of research findings on it (Carter & Mason, 1997). Nevertheless, curriculum integration is essential for the inclusion of marginalized information, such as the contents of peace education. The discussion here will feature its use in transformation-oriented pedagogy.

Building peace in a society, biosphere, and solar system has involved many aspects of conflict work that people in every discipline help to build as individuals, as well as specialists in their fields, and as members of an interdependent species (Kramer, 2011). While the focus of this book is on social education, the disciplines that are traditionally included as components of that field are particularly important topics. Table 4.1 displays those disciplines with examples of some of the challenges they are helping humans encounter.

TABLE 4.1 *Traditional disciplines of social education*

Discipline	Purview	Challenge Examples
Geography	How living and nonliving things affect each other	Sustainability, resources, and waste in outer space
Anthropology	Human origins, traits, and relations	Living in harm-free ways and interspecies relations
Sociology	Societal relationships and behaviors	Intergroup cooperation for problem solving
Psychology	Mental states and processes	Thought mediation and reframing of conflicts
Economics	Exchange of resources and services	Conscientious consumption and social banking
Political Science	Power relationships and government	Distribution of rights in the ecosphere and solar system
History	Record of time and events	Inclusive peace history and herstory across cultures
Humanities	The expressed qualities of being human	Illustration of humans interacting for peace

TABLE 4.2 *Emergent disciplines of social education*

Discipline	Purview	Challenge Examples
Multicultural education	Diversification of methods, content, and learning competencies	Use of intercultural knowledge and skills
Gender Studies	Gender understanding and accommodation	Equal representation and opportunities, incorporation of caring norms
Conflict and Peace Studies	Conflict sources, management, and preparation for peace	Identification of needs and fulfillment of them without harm

Table 4.2 Emergent disciplines that have been contributing to "curriculum transformation" with a peace orientation. James Banks (2014, p. 156) defines transformative curriculum as

> a curriculum that challenges the basic assumptions and implicit values of the Eurocentric, male-dominated curriculum institutionalized in U.S. schools, colleges and universities. It helps students to view concepts, events and situations from diverse racial, ethnic, gender and social-class perspectives. The transformative curriculum also helps students to construct personalized interpretations of the past, present and future.

Powerful instruction involving multiple and new disciplines necessitates connections.

Organizing for connections

There are foundational resources in schools for organizing transdisciplinary instruction. For example, the mission and vision statements of a school incorporate core concepts that can be used for planning. The values expressed in those documents are sources for concept-based instruction that facilitates student experiences across disciplines with each envisioned concept. Teaching social studies with big ideas, such as a universal concept, is an ongoing recommendation for organizing an inclusive curriculum for students with multiple types of learning needs (Lintner, 2012; Lintner & Schweder, 2011). Table 4.3 is an example of using the concept of peace for organizing instruction across subject areas. The table provides one of many possibilities for transdisciplinary learning with discipline-based viewpoints of one concept, peace.

My students, who are teacher candidates while others are seasoned educators, develop concept-based units every year. Both types of students have thought of many more ways to teach about peace within and across subject areas. In addition to subject-based lessons that illustrate those concepts operating in each discipline, they create plans for corresponding performance programs in which their students will demonstrate the concepts through the performing arts. In his book, *Schools of Hope*,

TABLE 4.3 *Concept-based learning within and across subject areas*

Subject	Concept Demonstration
History	Having multiple sets of data and viewpoints of an event to analyze its meanings and the roots of its conflict
Arts	Use of different media for expressing thoughts and feelings about conflict and peace
Language Arts	Many ways that language expresses power differences and changes in discourse that balance communication of power
Math	Balancing equations and use of math systems for that purpose in different languages and cultures
Science	Incorporating different ways of knowing about the material world to include contemplation and spirituality along with data analysis for resolving environmental conflicts
Health	Physical and social well-being while locally growing, eating, and trading food sources
Physical Education	Inclusive and cooperative fitness activities that accommodate special physical needs and incorporate diverse cultural norms

Heath (1994, p. 244) describes four schools that strived for coherent learning environments: "Each of the four schools of hope has a keynote, a predominant theme or vision, that integrates, though not perfectly, its learning environment. The vision contributes to a coherence in approach and programs that mutually reinforce each other's effects" (p. 244). The coherence of seeing a concept illustrated in every subject area involves imagination, unless students can participate in the actual functions of a discipline for applying that idea (Egan, 1992). A description of incorporating student rehearsal as preparation for a future function explains the role of imagery: "Imagination is a powerful adaptive skill. It helps us to anticipate, plan, and prepare in great detail and to practice and stabilize our plans without producing the irreversible consequences that occur when we must act in reality" (Heath, 1994, p. 249). Imagining a better society and teaching students about current issues has also provided an organizational structure for curriculum (Maebuta, 2011). Facilitating instruction about a social issue occurs across multiple subject areas (D'Ambrosio, 2008; Gross, Morton, & Poliner, 1993; Totten, 2012). Whether organizing the curriculum around a core concept or addressing societal issues separately in different subject lessons, visionary social education fosters aspirations to fulfill evident needs.

Meeting societal needs

Integration in social education can be facilitated through worldwide along with local foci that enable students' awareness of needs within and between societies (Grice, 2011; Seif, 2009; Shaban, 2012). Integration of conflict and peace topics across subjects facilitates those learning opportunities (Finley, 2011; International Network for Education in Emergencies, 2012). The interdependence of humans and their dependence on the resources of the earth are ideas that feature societal needs in the past, present, and future (Foster, 2009; Merchant, 2010; Nelson & Coleman, 2011; Wannawichitra et al., 2011). Unequal access to life- and culture-sustaining resources is an international as well as societal conflict that can be an organizing topic for instruction in all subject areas, besides in emerging disciplines like peace studies. Within separate subject lessons, students can identify domination and crime that is associated with resulting deprivation. Students have been learning that to understand and address needs in society they must listen to each other, not as enemies, but as humans who are connected in the task of constructing cultures of peace. Sharing their stories, awareness of different historical perceptions, and understandings of a societal conflict have accompanied the development of students' crucial listening skills (Bar-On & Adwan, 2006; Goldberg & Ron, 2014; Yogev, 2010). Having the skill to listen and hear the needs of others is both an individual as well as societal goal for achieving conflict transformation. Social education has also been organized with a focus on students' needs.

Meeting students' needs

Powerful instruction incorporates students' personal schema, cultural histories, and norms as well as the individual needs that their families and teachers recognize. Curriculum integration and adaptation have entailed responsive pedagogy in social education as well as in other subject areas (Meidl & Meidl, 2011). The contextual conditions of society, such as feelings of enmity resulting from recent and ongoing violence, affect the needs of the students and are determinants of pedagogy (Haavelsrud & Stenberg, 2012; Mustafa, 2011). Social education has met needs in such situations by bridging sectarianism via student integration and transformation of worldviews. For example, the integrated schools of Northern Ireland and other world regions where students witnessed intergroup violence have featured coexistence pedagogy and multiculturalism (McGlynn et al., 2004). Facility of a unity-based worldview and a culture of healing have been cornerstones of social education for students and their teachers (Danesh, 2006). Organizing the framework for all educational activities on a unity worldview and culture of healing was identified as a prerequisite of peace-oriented education in a former war zone (Danesh, 2006). Healing psychological wounds has been not only an identified need of students; it was specifically an organizing idea for a successfully used curriculum in post-apartheid South Africa (Maxwell, Enslin, & Maxwell, 2004).

Holistically, integration of all senses as well as norms in their use is a technique for stimulating learning of all students as well as those with special needs (Mucklow, 2009). Montessori emphasizes practical life skills for all ages in the curriculum. From early childhood motor skills through environmental and vocational capabilities of teen learners, Montessori incorporates many aspects of human life as meaningful instruction. Social interactions with the self and others in that holistic pedagogy are a natural aspect of those relevant lessons. Integration of spirituality in social education is not only holistic, as Montessori pedagogy has demonstrated, it is a very important aspect of the human experience that schools can incorporate through not only the history of humankind but also "the totality of the human experience connecting the past, linked to the present and looking ahead to the future" (National Council for the Social Studies, 2008, para. 9). An investigation of youth violence and citizenship found that "young people are looking for some form of spirituality and meaning in life" (Braungart & Braungart, 1998, p. 247). Spirituality integration incorporates another aspect of powerful social studies, besides being a component of holistic learning (Wickett, 2005). Spirituality is very meaningful in the lives of humans, whether or not they participate in religions. It is the task of social education to develop student knowledge about this meaningfulness (Miller, 2010).

Meaningful

Meaningful social education is relevant, in-depth, sequential, critical, reflective, and oriented toward the future as well as the present. Relevance in powerful social studies is crucial for rationalizing to students the curriculum and its facilitation. Students deserve to know why they will learn about selected topics and concepts. Planning of the relevance statements that will be made to students about why they will experience the selected curriculum content and learn particular skills provides a reflective step for the teacher during preparation of the instruction. Across all of my education courses that involve instructional planning, my students have shared with me the value of this reflective preparation they do for instruction. They have described their need to practice with thinking about how to link concepts of the past, current social realities, and possibilities for the future lives of their students. In their lessons about peaceful relations, my students often incorporate the concept of conflict in their rationale statements such as, *While we think about why people have responded to a conflict the way they did, we can contemplate and explore ways to resolve this type of conflict without harm. That awareness may help us build peace when that type of conflict occurs.* Thinking deeply enables the contemplation needed about the timeframes of the past, the present, and the future.

Depth of thought about selected topics, versus a diffusion of learning time for breadth of content coverage, allows students to build their "knowledge, skills, beliefs, and attitudes that are structured around enduring understandings, essential questions, important ideas, and goals" (National Council for the Social Studies, 2008, para. 7). The use of cultural universals has been one successful approach to providing meaningful instruction with opportunities to look in-depth at universal situations humans face (Brophy & Alleman, 2009). Cultural universals are basic human needs found in all societies to which all students can relate: "Regardless of their cultures, socioeconomic backgrounds, achievement levels, or special needs, so teachers can connect to these experiences as bases for developing historical, geographic, political, economic, sociological, psychological, or anthropological understandings" (Alleman, Knighton, & Brophy, 2007, p. 166). While deeply considering a situation that societies have, experienced learners can use multiple frameworks for asking questions and seeing the answers to them (Brown, 2011). For example, how does the farm field of tomatoes look to a person who is middle class, impoverished, homeless, a developer, farmer, fertilizer seller, migrant field worker, pesticide-sick employee, and so on? Multiple frameworks of what that crop represents epitomize the professions that social studies describes. The universal concept features relevance for English-language learners who can depict through the arts, if not yet describe in English, what the presented concept means to them and how they see humans interacting in it (Atkin, 1993; Pérez, 2002). The incorporation of the conceptions that newcomers share provides more than multiple frameworks for seeing, thinking about, and preparing to interact in situations. It accomplishes relevancy and the first stage of sequential learning.

The learning process begins with the exploration of student understandings and then expands their thinking. It depends on communication, through discourse, arts, and interactions, in an encouraging atmosphere the teacher maintains. The socially supportive milieu that has been recognized as crucial for the success of students with special needs and acquisition of a new language while receiving instruction in that acquired tongue also supports open communication by all students (Cruz & Thornton, 2013; Szpara & Ahmad, 2006). A classroom climate that feels safe enough for students to share their diverse perceptions of a situation in the past or present, and concerns about the future, is also conducive to critical discourse. Students need to feel that it is socially safe to critique power imbalances they can identify. The value of open criticism is not supported in every society and home environment. Hence, students will have varying degrees of participation in written and verbal discussions about power distribution and other sources of conflict. Additionally, their families and teachers' colleagues as well as administrators may not support that type of communication. Impediments to teaching critical discourse and other aspects of meaningful social studies have been widely identified (Patrick, 1986). However, there are recommendations for coping with and responding to those impediments. Taking time to build positive teacher and student relationships has helped (Washington & Humphries, 2011). Beyond partnership approaches to education that Eisler (2000) and Comer (2004) elaborate, strategic compliance and redefinition are helpful strategies (Cornbleth, 2002). Strategic compliance involves apparent compliance with dominant culture while teaching students to recognize conflicts and proactively respond to them. An example of this can be teaching multicultural and peace history that is not in the canon or in the provided curriculum (Boulding, 1992; Etzioni, 1991). Anchoring instruction to standards that rationalize teaching diverse perspectives and other components of critical analysis demonstrates strategic compliance. Strategic redefinition involves explanations of educational goals that incorporate the learning needs, such as how the students will understand and respond to conflicts in the future without harm. The felt need for peace is an evident value across societies.

Value-based

Powerful and visionary instruction reflects the values of the society, nation, and world while it enables students to clarify their own values. In other words, students learn the values their schools pass on in representation of its region and populations. More recently, schools also include global values as a component of social education. While encountering the values presented in the school, students use the individual, family, and cultural morals they have been developing in formation of their dispositions and responses to the instruction they experience. For example, when a student encounters a conflict in history and a current social issue, the response the student chooses for communicating about the problem will be influenced by interaction values (Oetzel & Ting-Toomey, 2013). Consequently, students will have different reactions to the social content of their lessons and sometimes the way they participate in it.

These situations are learning opportunities for everyone involved in the lesson due to the diversity of perspectives and manner of responding to content that students have. The different norms of responding to curriculum content enrich the multicultural awareness of students. During values-clarification activities students have the opportunity to think about the relationship among identities, values, and behavioral norms. Social-emotional awareness at the individual level has become a goal for education of youth. Awareness of feelings and identification of their sources in expressed differences of values is an aspect of social and emotional learning as well as an opportunity for communication with self and others about those feelings (Elias & Arnold, 2006; Elias et al., 2003; New York State Education Department, 2011). The values component of powerful social education gives students opportunities to learn communication strategies for expressions of feelings and thoughts. Carole Hahn (2012, p. 79) points out that during her teaching career, "it involved giving attention to content, pedagogy and climate." Finding ways to accommodate value differences is a challenge children and adults face in the quest for peaceful coexistence as a diverse community, nation, and world. Hence, opportunities for value recognition, clarification, and accommodations for the sake of peace now, as well as in the future, have rationale in the challenging component of powerful instruction.

Challenging

While teachers demonstrate their respect for students, they also promote the reflective and critical thinking that students need to develop as intellectual habits. Teachers can guide students to think about fulfillment of all needs in a conflict that can be discussed during informal as well as formal instruction. The challenge of meeting needs entails creativity, which is often a precursor to the harm-free conflict transformation that Galtung (2004) recommends. Fostering creativity in search of solutions to value and other types of conflict can occur in an open and accepting atmosphere which educators, other school staff, and students' families co-construct. The National Council for the Social Studies (2008, p. 13) has clarified the importance of adult modeling in facilitation of challenging education: "Teachers show interest in and respect for students' thinking and demand well-reasoned arguments rather than opinions voiced without adequate thought or commitment."

While educators can share with students their actions in response to conflicts and the values that underlie their deliberate activities within and outside of school, they must avoid promulgating sectarian or other divisive orientations. The National Council for the Social Studies (2008, p. 18) points out while engaged in those actions:

> teachers make sure that students: (a) become aware of the values, complexities and dilemmas involved in an issue; (b) consider the costs and benefits to various individuals and groups that are embedded in potential courses of action and (c) develop well-reasoned positions consistent with basic democratic social and political values.

It is important that teachers carefully plan their responses to students' queries about educators' own thoughts and actions, as well as the activities that might best stimulate awareness. With my students, I have found that asking them to help me understand a situation from different perspectives so that I could make a better-informed decision was effective in prompting their own thinking about multiple ways of seeing a situation. There are several ways, besides inviting students to help diversify viewpoints, of rendering challenging learning opportunities (Alleman & Brophy, 1994; Wade, 2007). Each one challenges the thinking of the students to stretch their knowledge and increase the flexibility of their mental capacities. That condition prepares them for responding to human interactions and working for improved relations. Enabling students to be active learners, versus passive vessels for storage of information, is also an aspect of powerful social studies.

Active

Comprehensive and active social education involves planning for the cognitive, emotional, and physical realms of student interaction as a community of learners and society. Intergenerational learning through action has been used for visionary social education (Ethridge & Branscomb, 2009). The cognitive goals include stimulation of higher-order thinking that avoids dichotomous analysis. Thinking that presents two positions in an issue with only those limited ways of seeing it is dichotomous thinking. When media and published curriculum provide information in dichotomies, students especially need other sources for acquiring diverse perceptions for their flexible thinking and analysis. Interacting with cognitive processes are the emotional states of students (Lemerise & Arsenio, 2000; Yablon, 2006). Planning for how students can identify and express their feelings, especially when they involve discomfort, is also an important consideration in social education. There is a need to identify emotions that constrain thinking, especially fear and enmity (Fritzsche, 2006). Examples provided in literature, music, and other media of how emotions have been recognized and transformed as initial steps for peace action can provide indirect instruction for social-emotional development and learning (SEL). For example, some of Linda Williams's songs help students learn to identify their feelings as an initial step of SEL and peace action. In her song *It's Ok to Feel* (1995) the lyrics point out the goal of avoiding harm as a response to anger. "So now I take that anger / And turn it into energy / To do someone some good!" While communication and arts have been crucial outlets and means of expression, time for contemplation and for releasing stress is vital to both cognitive and physical states of learners. Physical interaction, coupled with mental processes, provides not only holistic learning opportunities; it also offers more creativity through different ways of interacting with the instructional contents (Korn-Bursztzn, 2012). Use of tiered activities and choices for students to select how they will participate in the learning maximizes their opportunities to engage with the content and demonstrate their learning (Boyle-Baise & Zevin, 2009). With the theory of multiple intelligences, educators can design options for student participation (Gardner, 1993). For example, students can be encouraged to use two or more intelligences for demonstrating their thoughts and feelings. Subsequent to that reflection and communication about how they perceive and feel is student planning for right action that they believe would be best in response to a situation (Thornton, 2005). For example, after learning how music has been used in social protest to stimulate needed changes in society, students may decide to use that technique in their own school or community for bringing attention to a conflict they recognize (Pellegrino & Lee, 2012). Students need time to form their vision of societal conditions that would be conducive for peace. Social education has several ways of incorporating that component of powerful learning.

Visionary

Incorporation of visioning includes near and far futurism. The near future involves the lives of the students whereas the far future is generations that succeed them. Analysis of the past enables understanding of the present conditions and relations in the world. In addition, that awareness equips students with examples of mistakes to avoid making again. Analysis of future projections allows people to prepare in advance for and think about crises and how existing and future challenges might be proactively faced. The inclusion of possible futures in social education has been underdeveloped in the curriculum. While future prediction is an important tool for planning that professionals use, social educators have been seeking ways to engage their students in futurism (Hutchinson, 1996; Hutchinson & Herborn, 2012). In response to this need, Table 4.4 provides futurism with the instructional themes stipulated by the National Council for the Social Studies.

With an orientation toward the future, response to conflict is a focus of social education. Transdisciplinary education for peace optimally incorporates the goal of conflict transformation.

Transformation of conflict is a goal in the pursuit of peace. Improved interactions with self and others for better relationships are changes sought. The transformation vision shows improved relationships and the well-being of those who were connected in a conflict. The dimensions of intrapersonal, interpersonal, and structural conflict are all interdependent. Each of those dimensions is a strand of discipline-based lessons about conflict in formal and informal education (Carter, 2010a; Weaver & Biesecker-Mast, 2003). Hence, the multidisciplinary content of social education is prime for instruction about the opportunities students will have throughout their lives to manage conflict, regardless of which professional and personal paths they will take. For that purpose, students can participate in simulations wherein they act out the functions of each discipline and identify the three levels of conflict experienced in that work. As an example, a simulation involving the work of mediators involves intrapersonal and interpersonal communication that, when involving political contexts, can affect structural conflicts through the achievement of improved relations. Literature with peace history offers several examples of the three dimensions of conflict and transformations that focus on non-harmful relations. For instance, in *Chicken Soup for the Soul, Stories for a Better World* (Canfield et al., 2005), the accounts of presidents such as James Carter and Oscar Arias, along with those of many other people, feature inner thoughts, interactions, and the outcomes that avoided harm. All of the components of powerful

TABLE 4.4 *Futures contents in the themes of social education*

Themes	Futures Contents
Culture	Which aspects of your culture promote peace? How might different professions support a global culture of peace?
Time, Continuity, and Change	What would you change in your community to help its inhabitants live more peaceful lives? How will knowledge of peace history help politicians use their positions to fulfill needs in their region and others?
People, Places, and Environments	How can you live in your environment with minimal waste? What will people do to reduce or eliminate dependence on oil for fuel?
Individual Development and Identity	How will your personal and social skills in peace development affect your family, community, and world? How might your identity as a peace builder be important in an organization to which you belong?
Individuals, Groups, and Institutions	How will the institutions to which you belong change with their commitments to peace? What could each do to enact them?
Power, Authority, and Governance	How will you work to redistribute power to disadvantaged others? What decision processes will occur to avoid a dissatisfied minority?
Production, Distribution, and Consumption	What ways will you and your family avoid consumerism, which involves shopping for and purchasing unnecessary goods? How will people fulfill their life-sustaining needs with nearby resources?
Science, Technology, and Society	How will you decide what technology you need to live a peace-promoting life? What technologies can be created to build peace?
Global Connections	What changes will you make to support the well-being of people in other regions who are interdependent with you? How will prosocial consumption be encouraged and facilitated to support and protect the producers in other regions of goods that your community needs?
Civic Ideals and Practices	What will be your functions as a global and galactic citizen who builds peace everywhere that humans can reach? How will global citizens collaborate to improve life conditions for everyone?

learning fit into transdisciplinary lessons about peace in the past, the present, and the future. The What About Peace? program is a component of transdisciplinary learning that promotes students' answers to the title question through multiple modalities of arts and language usage (Global Exchange, 2014).

Conclusion

Visionary social education must be powerful while it is transdisciplinary. Curriculum designers and instructors have several components to incorporate for such broad and deep learning opportunities. Transdisciplinarity incorporates diverse ways of seeing and thinking about concepts and events that illustrate them. Changing cultural and disciplinary lenses that allow multiple viewpoints of lesson contents provide breadth. Enriching breadth is processing of the information in culturally different ways. Organizing instructional contents around concepts supports coherent and relevant instruction across subject areas, with the incorporation of emergent disciplines.

Adding power to student learning involves design of lessons that are integrative, meaningful, value-based, challenging, and active (Table 4.5). The addition of their visioning skills as a competency in powerful instruction orients students toward the future. Students can imagine their future

TABLE 4.5 *Case example*

Kids in Action
While learning about groundwater and sources of contaminants to it, the students at Jackson Elementary in Salt Lake City, Utah, became concerned. They wondered about, and then investigated, a nearby site that contained thousands of old barrels for possible recycle. After noticing on a visit to the site that the corroded barrels might be leaking chemicals into the ground and water supply, the students started reading newspaper and journal articles about hazardous waste. They felt a need to have the barrel site cleaned up. To accomplish that, they visited and communicated their wish to the city's mayor, who did get the task done within that school year.
However, the students then became aware of the negative impact on the owner of the recycle business full of old barrels. This stimulated their concern about other owners of similar enterprises who may not have the money to check for and remove sources of hazardous waste. Consequently, the students ran a fund-raising campaign in the next school year, through their letters to local businesses, to support cleanup of sites that might be contaminating groundwater. Without the legal right to give their collected funds to the health department for the needed work, the students pursued legislation. They even visited the State House on the day of the voting. The new bill, which was unanimously passed under the watchful eyes of the students, allowed government funding to clean up toxic waste sites.
Subsequent students at Jackson Elementary learned about funding sources and wrote matching grants to support needed reforestation. In that process, they realized that children in other areas could benefit from involvement in tree planting. Hence, they created a petition and lobbied for funds that children could use for such purposes. "Although Congress did not write a special bill for them, they did attach the idea to make money available for kids to the 'America the Beautiful Act of 1990'" (Lewis, 1998, p. 11).

TABLE 4.6 Interdependent workers

Lesson Plan
We Need Each Other

Lesson Goal
Students will comprehend the interdependence of workers in a community.
Exploration
Students identify many professions, representing multiple disciplines, that exist in their region.
Development
Students create a physical web of interdependence with yarn ends they hold in a circle as workers who depend on each other. They each have one task/job that workers need in order to do their jobs.
Expansion
In their different roles of workers, students respond to a hypothetical or historical conflict, such as an economic crisis, with their plan of maintaining the survival needs of all workers, in the same or different job roles.

without harmful responses to conflict and ways of living that avoid current problems (Table 4.6). Holistic learning that incorporates many aspects of psychological and physical experiences as humans enhances the creativity needed for problem solving. Conflict transformation involves the improvement of relations with self and others. The goal of better treatment is applicable in all realms of life and places where it can exist. Students who learn how to manage their thoughts and actions through intrapersonal processes, as a critical step toward interpersonal harmony, will be better equipped to make the structural changes that are needed in peace development.

Instructional opportunities. Plan for where in the curriculum you can fit the emergent disciplines of social education: multicultural education, gender studies, and conflict and peace studies. Demonstrate for students where each of these fit into the traditional disciplines of social education. Facilitate a unity world view by incorporating true stories about peace processes that include gender balance in examples from different world regions. Use and expand the futures contents in social education.

Curricular applications

1 Present to students the challenge examples of each discipline that social education traditionally includes. Plan opportunities throughout the school year for identification of how people are meeting those challenges. Describe how you would facilitate those opportunities.

2 Identify what in the vision and mission statements of multiple schools in your region are resources for organizing instruction. In which lessons might you use those statements as rationale for teaching students visionary lessons?
3 How can you create a socially supportive milieu in your class that fosters student sharing? Meaningful lessons that incorporate student sharing of their thoughts, experiences, and perceptions occur in a safe learning environment. Describe what provides the safety and comfort to students for that communication.
4 By what means will you facilitate values clarification of your students? Describe how they might develop accommodations in your class for differences of values.
5 What peace history will you include in your class for student analysis of values that they can discern in those events? How will you ensure they learn about peace in multiple cultures and regions?
6 What other theme, besides those provided in Table 4.4, might enhance visionary social education for peace? Write the questions that future content might include with that theme.

Resources for visionary learning

On the Internet

Academic Social Action Collective (http://www.asacollective.org/)
Collaborative for Academic, Social and Emotional Learning (http://casel.org/)

Literature

Atkin, S. B. (1993). *Voices from the fields: Children of migrant farmworkers tell their stories*. Boston, MA: Little, Brown and Company.
Canfield, J., Hansen, M. V., Carter, C. C., Palomares, S., Williams, L. K., & Winch, B. L. (eds). (2005). *Chicken soup for the soul: Stories for a better world*. Deerfield Beach, FL: Health Communications.
Gross, F. E., Morton, P., & Poliner, R. A. (1993). *The power of numbers: A teacher's guide to mathematics in a social studies context*. Cambridge, MA: Educators for Social Responsibility.
Pérez, L. K. (2002). *First day in grapes*. New York, NY: Lee & Low Books.

Totten, S., & Pedersen, J. E. (eds). (2013). *Educating about social issues in the 20th and 21st centuries: A critical annotated bibliography* (Vol. 2). Charlotte, NC: Information Age.

Glossary

Canon: the traditional body of information that has been provided in schools, which typically features dominant culture.

Enmity: the perception of someone or something as an enemy, which can result with hostility.

Social-emotional development and learning: education that enhances the social and emotional competencies of students.

Transdisciplinarity: a process of learning through different forms of knowledge.

Transformative curriculum: instructional content designed to change students' knowledge and world views.

Expansion

1 Identify the ways of knowing that you have participated as an individual as well as a member of one or more cultures. Describe what you are doing when your awareness becomes evident. What other ways of raising your awareness might you try? Think about contemplative practices used around the world to identify a different one for your experience.

2 For which disciplines do you feel a need to learn more about their roles in peace development? Make a list of them and include with it at least two ways each might, in the future, additionally improve the social and physical conditions for life.

3 What polarizes your viewpoints? Identify what in your past and present colors your perspective of human interactions. How can your awareness of what influences your perspectives help you enhance them in the future?

4 What evidence of interpersonal peace in cross-cultural contexts have you observed? How might interpersonal peace be enhanced in different professional situations, of different disciplines, through use of intrapersonal skills?

5 What is your vision of powerfully educated students who are prepared for a peaceful future? Describe what they are doing in their personal, professional, and public lives.
6 How do you see your own life becoming more peaceful in the coming decade? Describe the personal and professional aspects of your life that will reduce harm as a response to conflict.

5
Mindful and Engaged Citizenship

Abstract: *Citizen responsibility for immediate, regional, and global relations has a foundation of awareness, dispositions, and skills. Dispositions that support proactive responses to awareness of needs are mutuality, concern, stewardship, service, involvement, courage, and patience. Participatory skills enable proactive responses to conflict. In addition to awareness, supportive dispositions, and skills for civic participation, a positive vision of human relations stimulates active citizenship. Creative visioning processes include positive images of oneself and others, including the "other." Construing peace builds crucial hope. Engaged citizenship for peace has social, environmental, ethical, geographic, economic, and political realms for student visioning, planning, and involvements.*

Carter, Candice C. *Social Education for Peace: Foundations, Teaching, and Curriculum for Visionary Learning.* New York: Palgrave Macmillan, 2015.
DOI: 10.1057/9781137534057.0009.

Citizenship foundations

Peace in our interdependent world depends on comprehensive citizenship. Citizenship entails responsibilities that one has as a member of humanity. Comprehensive citizenship has several contexts in which people have caretaking responsibilities. Responsibility for immediate, regional, as well as global relations has a foundation of awareness, dispositions, and skills. Supportive dispositions for comprehensive citizenship motivate responses to awareness. Participatory citizenship skills enable proactive responses. In addition to awareness, supportive dispositions, and skills for civic participation, a positive vision of human relations stimulates active citizenship. Aspiration for, and conceptions of, peaceful interaction in this violent world are catalysts of prosocial citizenship. Prosocial efforts have a goal of well-being.

The awareness, dispositions, skills, and vision that are aspects of participatory citizenship develop in several contexts. Informally, as well as formally, teachers demonstrate and teach about citizenship. Through their own proactive citizenship about which the students are aware, and across strands of social studies, teachers provide formal and informal education. Therefore, teaching and learning citizenship is wide ranging within school and beyond because it has many opportunities for experiential learning. Engaging citizenship education enables student application of their knowledge and skills while they develop supportive dispositions and a positive vision.

Awareness

There are many contexts for attention to citizenship. Students learn that their membership in groups involves responsibilities in each. As a member of a family, identity group, school, organizations, community, region, global humanity, biosphere, and larger contexts, there is a need for attention to one's individual and collective influence on well-being. With the expanding environment method of social education, students learn first about their most immediate influence in their home and neighborhood. From there, educators broaden students' awareness of several other contexts of human and interspecies interdependence, bringing attention to the ripple effect of personal and local decisions (Andrzejewski, Pedersen, & Wicklund, 2009). For example, students learn how their interaction with people in their family, social groups, and community can be improved with the expression of care, especially in the midst of conflict. By looking for the underlying need that conflict reveals, identification of its source is an important step toward problem solving that supports the maintenance of the group. Additionally, students discover how ecological actions affect local as well as global well-being.

The first place to look, and sometimes the least obvious, for sources of conflict is within. Intrapersonal peace is the first responsibility everyone has. Questions help with the identification of a felt conflict: *What is bothering me? What do I need now, and later?* Students learn that maintaining mindfulness of one's own mental and physical state is crucial for managing it (Song & Muschert, 2014).

> Mindfulness, or mindful awareness, is the moment-to-moment process of actively and openly observing one's body and mind. Science has shown that mindfulness can address stress, depression, anxiety, boost the immune system, work with chronic pain, improve attention, and create a general sense of wellness and well being. It has also been shown to impact focus, learning, behavior, and wellness in school children. (Mindfulness Awareness Research Center, 2008)

A sane and responsible citizen knows how to manage extreme emotions until the mind can return to normal, thereby protecting oneself and others from harmful actions. In schools, students can learn relaxation techniques and harmless outlets for their emotions (Burke & Hawkins, 2012). Throughout my career in primary and secondary teaching, relaxation activities following transition time and field trips were useful for activation of student mindfulness and conflict de-escalation. Prosocial music is one method of helping students learn about actions that they can take when they feel intense emotions (Carter, 2003). The song "If You're Angry and You Know It" by Linda Williams (1996), which she wrote in the grip of emotions after her family member was robbed and murdered, helps students learn that their first task is recognizing and finding a harmless outlet for their intense feeling. They learn that displacement of anger, whereby they hurt someone or something else, is counterproductive for problem solving. Students need awareness that harm to anything has extensive effects, described as ripples. Needed are ripples of internal peacemaking that positively affect the self and others (Figure 5.1).

In his efforts to transform difficult structural conflicts, José Martí once observed that "I must, begin within myself, see myself through myself"

Mindful and Engaged Citizenship 95

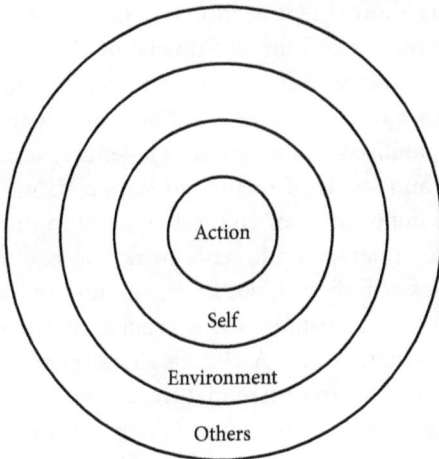

FIGURE 5.1   *Ripples from our actions*

(Cardoso, 1997, p. 170). Stated another way, *I must see how what I am and have experienced affect my thoughts and reactions.* This form of self-awareness facilitates understanding of why we as individuals have reactions that are different from those of others to the same situations. When one has lived with long-term conflict of any type, there are psychological and physical responses that occur. Without recognition and management of those responses, they have greater effect on interactions. However, some of those initial reactions can be valuable for raising awareness among others about conflicts.

The second place to look for sources of conflict is the interactions between people. At a very early age, students observe, and sometimes copy, discriminatory behavior predicated on deep-seated perceptions of people. Mindfulness of human interaction involves alertness to thoughts about, and responses to, people. It is intentional, experiential, and non-judgmental. "It allows us to see things as they are without a mental assignment of critical labels to our thoughts, feelings, and perceptions" (Williams et al., 2007, p. 48 in Hyland, 2014). Recognition of internal prejudicial thinking and bias needs self-mediation. It is the crucial step of monitoring one's own interactions (Walsh, 1997). Mediating the self involves listening to the inner voice when responding to internal questions such as: *What does this other person need from me? How would I want to be treated if I were that person? Am I being respectful and fair? How can I adapt to the way that person communicates differently than me?*

Internal dialogue allows identification of a negative conception about another, which shows a need for self-mediation. Most often, the need for such monitoring occurs in situations with identity group differences. Identity differences have several sources including social class, ethnic, religious, cultural, ability (versus disability), gender, sexual orientation, linguistic factors, and levels of formal education. James Banks (2008) reminds us of the importance of cultural citizenship that includes how people respond to, interact with, and work for equitable treatment of others, regardless of their identity. Awareness of how any group experiences difficult circumstances is a crucial citizenship foundation (Crocco, 2000; Heafner, 2008). A simple global perspective overlooks how experiences vary due to differential treatment, while a transformative one recognizes diverse areas of need. With a transformative global perspective, students develop awareness. Looking back at the ripple, students can see how when someone ignores, or aids another, there can be a missed opportunity or far-reaching effect.

A difference in goals is a common source of interpersonal conflict. Mindfulness includes awareness of others' goals and corresponding needs. This often occurs through reframing; or viewing a conflict from a different perspective. Communication as well as research skills facilitate discovery of the needs others express and how they are trying to fulfill them. Lyrics learned in the song "I'll Listen" by Patricia Mikkelson (2008) help recall inner and outer communication processes during conflict. With compassionate communication techniques, inoffensive conversations occur for problem analysis in the midst of conflict (Rosenberg, 2003/2005). For analysis of widespread conflict, research facilitates awareness and understanding.

The third place to look for sources of conflict are in the systems which present problems for particular or whole groups of people. Commonly compared in social education are the variable participation rights of citizens in different political systems. In addition to that knowledge, students need to learn about current, as well as past, economic and social structures that interfere with human rights (Amnesty International, 2005/2007; Bigelow, 2008). For example, students in developed nations learn about how production of goods in underdeveloped regions relates to their own lifestyles (Hursh & Ross, 2000). They learn to ask: *Who made this product, and what were the conditions of that labor? For healthy living, were they adequately paid for and protected during that work? Did they have the freedom to choose the work they did, or were they forced into it? How did their identity affect their work options? How can we respond to their needs?* Conversely, questions by those who are victims of systemic violence in production are: *What do the consumers know about how this work is done? How are we constructively informing consumers of the oppression we are experiencing? What can we do to give them information about this problem? Who can help us get this information to the consumers?* Beyond knowledge of political policies that affect well-being, students learn to recognize personal as well as international interdependence. They identify structures and their role in them. To facilitate understanding of multidimensional conflicts, educators plan with this question in mind: "To what extent is the study of human life connected to the community, to all other life forms, the biosphere and the planet?" (Hart & Hodson, 2004, p. 178). Ultimately, breadth of awareness entails analysis of intrapersonal, interpersonal, and systemic conflicts as well as one's personal responsibility for responding to them. With awareness of systemic conflicts and violence, proactive responses result from, as well as inculcate, dispositions that support peacemaking.

Supportive dispositions

Attitudes cultivated in visionary social education enable peacemaking and peacebuilding. Dispositions that support proactive responses to conflict have four interactive processes that are depicted in Figure 5.2.

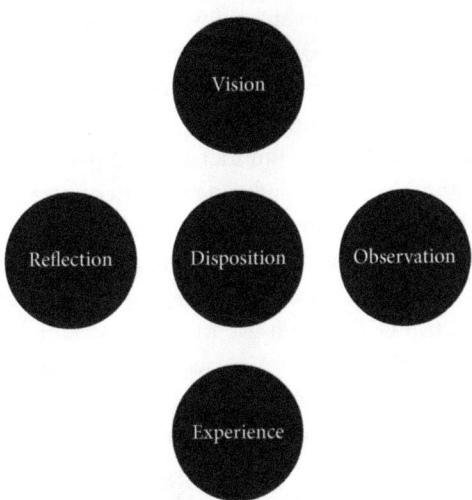

FIGURE 5.2 *Components of disposition development*

Attitudes are one of the greatest learning challenges in social education, and they are pivotal in civic participation. While contributing to one's awareness, dispositions also result from observations and experiences. Watching the behaviors and corresponding dispositions of others influences one's own attitude toward those who are facing each other in a conflict. Such observations by students occur in real-life situations as well as with illustrations of human interaction they encounter in media, literature, and art (Lonberger & Harrison, 2008; Pirtle, 1998; Spurgeon, 1998). For example, young students develop the disposition of empathy through facilitation of expressions about feelings in a conflict. With a vocabulary of feeling words, they learn to describe their own feelings and those of others. Formulated statements such as the following help them express feelings: "*How do you feel? Do you feel [feeling] about [context]?*" The disposition of concern for others as well as for self can be cultivated in many situations by school personnel and students' families.

Many venues for recognizing and identifying peace-promoting, and peace-undermining, dispositions are instructional opportunities. Educators use those venues as curriculum with cases for students to study. Instructors can teach students critical analysis of media and other observed contexts of conflict by asking questions about who has power and how lack of it affects dispositions (Apple, 1995; Cortés, 2000). In those lessons, students identify peoples' dispositions and their effects in escalation or de-escalation of conflict. Reflection on dispositions is an important process of self-awareness that can positively influence attitudes and corresponding behaviors. In his explanation of the need for restraint and analysis of negative thoughts and emotions, Bstan-'Dzin-Rgy (2001, p. 82), the Dalai Lama, points out that "the undisciplined mind is like an elephant. If left to blunder around out of control, it will wreak havoc. But the harm and suffering we encounter as a result of failing to restrain the negative impulses of mind far exceed the damage a rampaging elephant can cause." While living as a refugee in a foreign land, during which continual state-sponsored violence occurred in his homeland of Tibet, the Dalai Lama used much restraint from development of negative dispositions. As a displaced political leader faced with injustice, he exemplified self-control to avoid harm. With self-mediation of their thoughts about something observed, students identify their perspective and attitude. Cultivation of that skill occurs through practice with multiple perspectives, reframing, and awareness expansion. For example, students who have little or no experience with social groups in which they do not have membership typically lack a feeling of mutuality with the "other." Past or present conflicts between identity groups enlarge that void of affinity. Sustained positive experience with, and open reflection about, the "other" is the most common method used for cultivation of mutuality and elimination of negative viewpoints (Carter, 2005).

Here it is important to point out that short-term interaction with others who have been perceived as hostile to one's identity group are ineffective for positive transformation of negative attitudes. Educators must be aware that short-term interaction can reinforce negative perceptions (Moaz, 2002; Tomovska, 2009). Hence, teachers create maximum opportunities for their own, as well as students', sustained positive interaction with the "other." Such engagements enable ongoing communication that can facilitate understanding and a sense of commonality. Outside of those engagements, development of reflection habits that hold peace as criteria for evaluating inner thoughts can help students identify their own negative attitudes (Sommerfelt & Vambheim, 2008). Young pupils who lack such analysis skills have been able to reframe their perspective of situations. One concrete approach to that is providing pupils with clear or colored glass spectacles to wear as they look at a situation from another viewpoint. At the very least, the pupils learn the importance of reframing their perspective of conflict. This behavior can cultivate the disposition of concern, as well as result from it.

Dispositions can result from, as well as precede, prosocial behaviors. Hence the importance of modeling the dispositions and skills we want students of all ages to learn. All of the dispositions identified in this book as valuable for peace development can be modeled by teachers, which include Mutuality, Concern, Stewardship, Service, Involvement, Courage, Commitment, and Patience. Practice with such modeling enhances citizenship as well as teaching skills.

Skills

Citizenship encompasses skills in several contexts of civic engagement. Through mindfulness with a vision of peaceful interaction, citizens can maximize their awareness about conflicts and monitor their dispositions toward those who are involved in them. Seeing conflict from several different perspectives can help people understand these skills. The skill of non-dichotomous problem analysis is very important in development of needed knowledge. That skill is a challenge when text, media, or direct communication about a problem reduces perspectives of it. Too often, oversimplified polarities occur as information presents "right" and "wrong" value perspectives. When students identify and diagram in a T-Chart dichotomous presentations of information, they see the two-sided limitation of the information. That technique reveals the need for more perspectives of, and possibilities for, solving the problem. In the pursuit of information, a goal of obtaining more than two perspectives of a problem and its possible solutions helps students overcome the preponderance of oversimplified presentations about civic issues. A triangulation process (Figure 5.3), which identifies at least three different perspective angles of a problem, is a skill students learn for their research on issues.

Enabling that research requires preparation through multiple sources of information. Consequently, educators must find such sources, which can include noncommercial media and interviews or other communication opportunities for witness reports. Discussion with those who are directly experiencing a social issue provides insightful information. Involvement with adults in collection of such information builds students' skills in citizenship engagement. Students' knowledge, dispositions, and skills may influence adults' actions in those collaborations.

Partnership with others of different ages and cultures enriches citizenship skills as well as knowledge. It also can aid civic participation through collective actions. Students can team up with peers, near and far, in other grade levels for cross-age experiences in civic projects as well as in school governance through participation in groups, such as student councils and mediation programs. Organizations like the World Movement for Democracy (2014) and Ashoka's Youth Venture (2014) feature resources for and stories about civic projects by youth of different ages

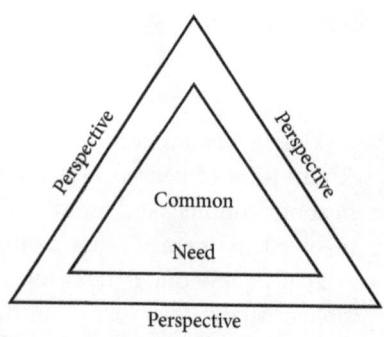

FIGURE 5.3 *Perspective triangulation*

and backgrounds. Learning with available members of the community, such as retired seniors, provides several opportunities for enhancement of student awareness as well as develops skills. Beyond learning about partnership relations in school-based and common-interest groups, students need skills of compassionate communication and cooperation with those who have different views and life experiences. The song "It's Us against the Problem, Not Me against You" (Williams, 1996) helps students remember that those experiencing a conflict with them are their "peace partners," no matter how many differences they perceive in their problem situation. Legitimizing another who has a different awareness and viewpoint involves active listening in that partnership. Learning how to validate the point of view, narrative, and aspirations of a Peace Partner is a developmental skill, which compassionate communication facilitates. For that purpose, students learn to ask clarification questions including: *You feel...about...? You need...?* During the clarification of needs, sources of conflict, including insidious violence, can become evident.

Analysis of information can help develop the skill of critical consciousness. Critical consciousness occurs through analysis of information (Freire, 1973). With that cognitive skill, students learn ways of distinguishing whose needs are not being fulfilled, and how, when they examine a conflict and its antecedents. This facilitates both national and cosmopolitan citizenship in conflict analysis (Darling, 2002). Being a member of a universal community comprised of an international society involves cosmopolitan citizenship (Linklater, 1998). Identification of how systems cause inequity and who is being served by those systems are crucial skills in the analysis of structural conflicts. Students learn, for example, identification of responses to gender and ethnic identity that indicate conflicts in their community and elsewhere (Au, Bigelow, & Karp, 2007; Reardon, 2001). With awareness of how injustice occurs, students use communication skills to plan and carry out actions in response to those conflicts (Kreisberg, 1992; Wade, 2007). After their identification of conflict sources, they can incorporate the domains of those problems in their vision of peace.

Vision

People tend to picture peace within their own perspectives, based on their prior experiences and their own values. Mindfulness incorporates breadth of vision for inclusiveness of self and others, including the "other." While clarity of processes that might manifest peace for everyone is not essential in vision cultivation, a maintained goal for the outcome of those engagements is very important (Boulding & Boulding, 1995; Hicks, 2004). One successful process has been the mental suspension of the presence as the initial step of imagining. It frees the imagination and, "enables the mind to leap over those local impossibilities that loom so large in the present" (Boulding, 1992, p. 211).

Creativity and flexibility in picturing peace processes and outcomes have been very valuable (Dryzek, 2005; Galtung, 2004). Youth are often less constricted in imaging possible solutions to problems. Consequently, they need opportunities to envision themselves in multiple engagements of peace-oriented problem solving and peaceful lifestyles (Figure 5.4). The cultivated vision includes self as a participatory citizen and collective action in pursuit of the good.

The arts have always been valuable for human expression of peace visions as well as illustration of conflicts. Students use graphic and performing arts to learn about how others have expressed visions of peace in addition to creating their own art works for that purpose (Catterall, 2007; National Center for Conflict Resolution Education, 2002; The Dalai Lama Foundation, 2006). Arts expression and story writing facilitate students' conceptions of peace with self and others. Images of peace

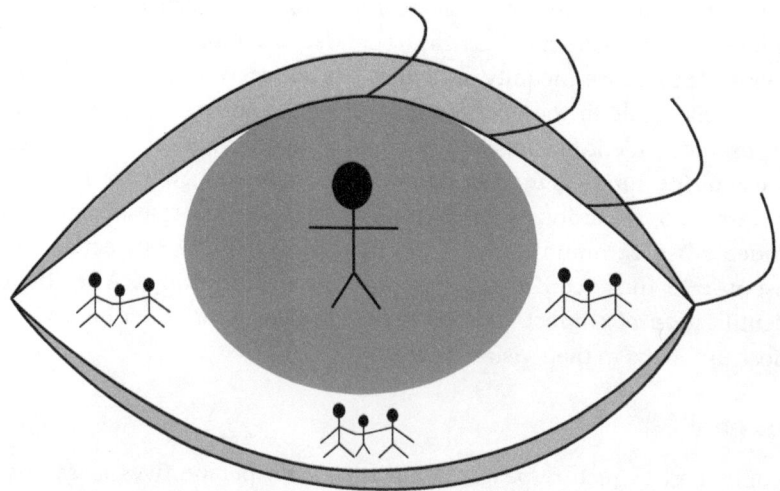

FIGURE 5.4   *Envisioning peace*

and processes of obtaining it will vary in their artistic productions due to contextual and cultural factors as well as the extent of students' capacities for imagining. Nevertheless, expressions of their peace conceptions provide valuable information for stimulating the interest and possible understanding of their educators, families, and friends. Students' visionary artwork reveals their perspectives of life situations and their ideas about possibilities for improving them.

Conceptions of and aspirations for peaceful interaction in this often-violent world can stimulate prosocial citizenship. Efforts to improve human relations along with collective well-being demonstrate prosocial citizenship. Construing peaceful contexts expresses hope and is a crucial step toward making needed changes in the students' lives, in the community, and in the world. Where existing violence has been pervasive or overwhelming, hope can seem difficult to cultivate. In his recognition of that situation, Daisaku Ikeda (2014) continually points out that gloom in the face conflict can be valuable. "Hope that has not been tested is nothing more than a fragile dream. Hope begins from this challenge, this effort to strive towards an ideal, however distant it may seem" (Ikeda, 2005, p. 22). Nobel Laureate Jane Goodall (2005, p. 11) provides the following four reasons for hope:

1 Humans are a unique problem-solving species because we are capable of linking
2 our sophisticated brains and *hearts* to create ingenious solutions to our problems.
3 The earth and its inhabitants are resilient when we work at repairing damages and
4 saving life forms.
5 There is an indomitable human spirit that enables groups of people to succeed
6 together on making seemingly impossible changes.
7 Young people have much energy for making change, once they understand the
8 nature of the problems.

Additionally, St. Augustine explained that the offspring of hope is courage; courage to make changes that are needed. With encouragement to bring about their visions of peace, youth have been successful in making needed changes to solve problems around the world. Jessica Rimington (2013), the founder and director of the One World Youth Project and who connects youth in action projects, was a student who summoned courage to work through an exclusion effort at a youth summit. In the process of transforming that conflict, she recognized the need for changing the disconnection between youth throughout the world, which hinders cross-cultural understanding and sustains systemic conflict. In her vision of peacebuilding as a student and global citizen, Jessica recognized the multiple places and people one action affects. Educators stimulate student visions of present and future conditions of peace in multiple domains.

Strands of citizenship

Mindful and engaged citizenship includes awareness of, involvement in, and a vision of peaceful interaction in several domains. Beyond the scope of political participation are the social, environmental, ethical, geographic, and economic realms of civic engagement.

Social citizenship

Students learn about their opportunities for participating in as well as understanding and communicating about interactions that shape their social world. In the social domain of citizenship are circumstances that can lead to positive human interactions students promote. With the cultivated disposition for equitable and fair treatment of everyone, students learn about opportunities for bringing that about. For that purpose, teachers provide instruction that facilitates student awareness of more than human differences, similarities, and common needs (Cleary & Peacock, 1998; Diller & Moule, 2005; Nieto, 2004). They enable student recognition of power differences between people that are sources of conflict. Learning about who has power and who does not in a micro or macro context occurs with critical pedagogy (Kincheloe, 2005; Weil, 1998). Students learn identification of conflicts that underlie interactions between groups and individuals of different identities with variable rights and privileges. With awareness of current inequitable opportunities, the disposition of concern, the skill of commitment, and the vision of a fair society, students can make and carry out a plan of action (Larson & Ovando, 2001). Such plans include bringing attention to the inequality and its sources, which can build a foundation for transformation and formation of problem-solving responses. In both types of student reactions, teachers recognize what skills need development for optimizing the success of their peacemaking efforts. For example, students often do not know how to engage in formal discourse through oral and written communication with organizations and officials. Peer conferencing in civics lessons hones needed discourse skills through conversations about civic actions (Anderson & Lubig, 2012). In the same vein, they may need assistance with cross-cultural communication skills, especially with the "other" in their community who had previously been avoided (Dresser, 1996). Purposeful peacemaking through encounters with the "other" are optimal when students first clarify their feelings, expectations, and goals. Such mindfulness aids in recognition of their needs during new encounters, which include awareness of their emotions and how they affect their ability to understand as well as listen. Students can ask themselves: *How well am I listening to this person? What can I do to show respect in this situation? What can I say to show understanding of this person's feelings and needs?* To summarize, visionary social citizenship involves skill with intrapersonal and interpersonal interaction, including multicultural competencies, in addition to awareness of and concern about the sources of social conflicts. Knowledge about past, present, and future environments augments social citizenship.

Environmental citizenship

As an aspect of environmental literacy, students learn about their responsibility for interactions in the environment and outcomes of them as members of the natural world (Basile, White, & Robinson, 2000). Comprehensibly, they learn to recognize how social conflicts derive from ecological problems, and how they compound them. For example, competition for resources and social discrimination underlie the problem of displaced and landless people. Racism in political and economic policies has been evident throughout the world, and it continues to be discernible in current trends. In his discussion about the relationship of peace and place, Nabhan (2007, p. 345) points out that "for too long we have assumed that confronting racism and social injustice were altogether different challenges from safeguarding land rights, practicing multigenerational land stewardship or protecting cultural and biological diversity." Education about the environment must no longer be separated from awareness of social experiences that are associated with ecological change. While students may recognize social outcomes of local ecological actions, they need information about distant impacts of those occurrences, the far-reaching ripples from their behaviors. The domains of citizenship and subjects of formal education are highly connected, which students can recognize in holistic instruction about environmental citizenship.

Across the curriculum, students use the skills of many subject areas for analysis and ultimate understanding of environments (Butzow & Butzow, 1999). They learn how human interaction has impacted environments in reciprocal ways. In cultivating a vision of a peaceful world, environmental education presents to students past and current challenges of resource restoration and management to which multiple social movements and individual endeavors have been responding. Simulations are learning experiences that prompt use of skills in many subject areas when they enact responses to conflict. Students take the different roles of people who have an interest in the conflict the simulation presents. The simulation *Trouble in Tortuga!* (Emerson, Movius, & Merideth, 1999) is an example of an environmental conflict resulting from development that might encroach sensitive habitat.

Awareness of the breadth of those initiatives helps envisioning multidimensional peace for all life (Gottlieb, 2002). Students discover that their participation in environmental restoration and caretaking as individuals and as members of groups are crucial for pursuit of their goal. While dealing with setbacks in those pursuits, they learn to reflect on both their goals and the means they are taking to accomplish them. Such mindfulness precedes identification of alternative means that may better fit the situation. It also reveals unity in the diversity of ways people approach social changes. In consideration about the range of environmental actions people take, it became evident that

> it looks like a bunch of static at first. But if you look deeply enough you see that there's a coherency—people taking different approaches, but for the same aspirations: so that we have healthy communities, and people's daily work can be adding to the health of their communities and ecosystems. (Jones, 2007, p. 57)

Anthony Kapel "Van" Jones (2007), a White House environmental advisor, civil rights activist, and attorney who founded several nonprofits, knows the need for self-work as well as collective work for bringing about change. Like Mohandas Gandhi and his predecessors, Jones points out that "we have to confess and accuse, we have to be able to look within and without, fight for changes both in society and within ourselves"

(p. 61). Transforming language usage to eliminate violence terminology is one of many ways activists work on habit change in the pursuit of peace. Developing a multicultural nonviolent language environment for optimal social education is a deep change (Bowers, 1993). Pluralizing ways of knowing beyond rationality based on "factual" evidence accomplishes another deep change. In learning about different cultural ways of knowing, students can analyze representations of humans and nature. With literary and visual depictions, students discern humans illustrated as owners and managers of their ecological world (Bowers, 2001; Minteer & Taylor, 2002). Whether the curriculum is formal in textbooks or informal in media they encounter, students learn to ask: *Where are the rights in this situation? Who and what has those rights?* In answering those questions, students can consider nature, humans, and spirits as well as deities while they examine the dilemmas of human dominance in and destruction of the natural world. Through that analysis, students detect obstacles to ecological preservation and restoration.

Obstacles to ecological maturity are moral invisibility, ecological illiteracy, lifestyle rigidity, and politics (Bendik-Keymer, 2006). When obscured from moral visibility, humans cannot see other life forms as worthy of respect through rights to a healthy life. Instead, other life forms are viewed as resources for human use in any way, or just their disposal. Culture influences the degree of the rights viewpoint. To understand how such beliefs developed, students learn about the historical context of cultures that evidence moral invisibility before they create awareness-raising possibilities for people of those cultures. The maturity that supports environmental well-being is evident in ecological literacy, which is the ability to read the needs of the environment, and comprehension of its preservation requirements. Without ecological literacy, humans make unwitting mistakes due to their lack of awareness about what is needed. Students can identify ecological needs in their environment and other regions which their lifestyles impact. Lifestyle rigidity of humans associates with ecological literacy. People have habits that need to quickly change for environmental care. With identification of their habits that need changing, students can support each other in the accomplishment of those lifestyle transformations. Economic pressures to sustain current employment modes contribute to the rigidity problem. After identifying the environmental impact human work has, students can recommend conversion or elimination of production modes that negatively affect an environment (Daly & Farley, 2004). Finally, the politics of changing whole societies' norms to eliminate destructive effects on nature is a large obstacle. With awareness of peace history, how humans have transformed structural conflicts without the use of violence, students can plan as well as recommend collective actions that have been effective in making policy changes. For instance, with ecological democracy, in which environments as well as people have representation, students work for representation of a deteriorating ecosystem (Dryzek, 2005).

In comprehensive citizenship education, students find opportunities for overcoming these four obstacles. Jeremy Bendik-Keymer (2006) posits that learning to use moral perception, ecological literacy, moral creativity, and political-economic liberty, one can clear the pathways to environmental citizenship. Those paths are far-reaching and come with ethical signs to read on the journey of humankind. In his *Letter from a Birmingham Jail*, Martin Luther King Jr. (1963, para. 4) pointed out that "injustice anywhere is a threat to justice everywhere. We are caught in an inescapable network of mutuality, tied in a single garment of destiny. Whatever affects one directly affects all indirectly." The mantra "Act globally and think locally" reminds us that we need to think about broad contexts, such as nature, and then work where we are to improve conditions (Lipietz, 1995). Such improvements are intentioned for realization of *the good*.

Ethical citizenship

Students learn about individual and collective responsibility for ethical interactions that support well-being. Imaging *the good* life for all members of a society helps people identify acceptable and unacceptable behavior. Clarification of what *the good* includes helps with visioning of its enactment in society (Bellah et al., 1991; Donnison, 1995). While cultivating their mindfulness, students learn about value differences that underlie disagreements in what people construe as moral thinking and behavior. With that awareness and vision, students clarify what values they have, which align with their supportive dispositions, in pursuit of peace (Sawatsky, 2008). Their disposition of pluralism, which holds everyone in a society as a worthy member, is in their vision of people with different identity groups living together as they work through conflicts. Students can examine their personal viewpoint of societal members and see how negative perceptions of any identity group affect their active or passive behaviors around members of that group. Considering situations of injustice facilitates that viewpoint-outcome analysis (Percoco, 2001). When someone of a different identity group is being treated poorly, students can ask: *Is that how everyone (or everything) should be treated in this society? Is it how I want to be treated? Why does identity matter here?* Those questions are not limited to the topic of humans.

Comprehensively, ethical citizenship occurs through pursuit of the good for all living beings, not just humans. During a return to the practices of indigenous cultures that recognize all life forms as holders of spirit, which are worthy of honor, societies are now increasing their examination of ethical behavior with animals and other life forms (Wangoola, 2006). Interspecies relations are important considerations that have been documented in laws which protect the rights of animals. Other initiatives are giving recognition to nature, as a whole in rights for enactment of *the good* (Minteer & Taylor, 2002). Eco-justice conveys the conception of Nature's rights. Ecuadoreans, for instance, used democracy to vote on whether or not to give Nature equal rights under the law (Kendall, 2008). Concern for sustainability on earth also propels the trend toward protection of nature. Lessons about contextual sustainability facilitate a bio-centric world view in which humans are one of many life forms in a web of interdependence (Verhagen, 2004). Concern about survival on earth and human interactions beyond it evidence the breadth of comprehensive citizenship (Wenden, 2004). Standards that humans develop for enactment of *the good* in the pursuit of peace extend beyond earth to all of the places where humans or their tools have reached.

Geographic citizenship

Students learn that citizenship includes their membership in locations that are far away, as well as near (Peters & Britton, 2008). They have communal, national, international, and galactic spheres of influence. Consequently, their responsibilities are extensive and include mindfulness of how they impact life everywhere in a relationship of interdependence. While humans interact beyond the biosphere of earth, they have responsibilities in the galactic web of being. The citizenship role in humanity's frontier of outer space includes all of the other domains of civic responsibility, regardless of ethnic or national identity. While involving the other domains of citizenship, students consider who is doing what in outer space and how that might affect other beings, human or otherwise. Movements to protect outer space, for example, evidence concern about nuclear waste and human weaponry (Global Network against Weapons and Nuclear Power in Space, 2008).

Social, environmental, ethical, economic, and political aspects of an issue in any location need personal and collective responses. As students become aware of one of those five components of an issue, others become discernible. During examination of buying "cheap" shoes, students learn about how that action relates to social and economic injustice, political processes such as trade agreements which impede equal rights to fair-wage employment, unethical treatment of labor organizers, and environmental sustainability (Reardon, 1995). To enhance their awareness and comprehension of issues, students can use webbing and other graphic methods of depicting the connections between the domains of citizenship. Division of the domains to different students' groups for collaborative research and depictions of relationships can help them see the connections between each domain. Students follow up on identification of the multi-dimensional problem with mindfulness about their vision of peace, *the good* for everyone, and their conceptions of how that might occur. Their multi-dimensional depiction of that peace is a creative process that can be crucial to identification of needed actions (Shank & Schirch, 2008). As comprehensive-minded citizens, students know they are personally and collectively responsible for transforming and resolving conflicts they identify. Awareness of how people like themselves are being negatively affected by human behaviors that can change, such as consumption choices, motivates students' transformative actions. Students in Montclaire, New Jersey, sang Fair Trade Carols during the winter holidays around stores (Global Exchange, 2008). They were motivated by a positive impact they hoped to have on workers, including children, who produced the products the holiday shoppers might buy.

Economic citizenship

Students learn about economic systems and roles in them (Table 5.1). Although government standards for education have not promoted examination of major issues like federal debt, those topics are components of visionary curriculum (Marri et al., 2012). Comprehensive lessons for students mitigate the imbalance of civics texts that feature civil and political rights with less attention to social and economic rights (Avery & Simmons,

2000). Beyond an industrialized world view that sees materialism as valuable, students can think about their basic life needs and the effects of consumerism in their own lives. A critical pedagogy of consumption enables analysis of the relationship among production, popular culture, and consumption as social behavior (Sandlin et al., 2009; Shor, 2004). Reflection on "having and being," which teachers as well as religious leaders of different faiths facilitate, enables awareness of how possessions divide more than unite people (Fromm, 1979). In that reflective process, students can ask themselves: *How does what I have cause separation? Why do I have things that separate me from others?* Through guided reflection and media literacy, students can see how they are influenced by a commercial portrayal of being. With awareness of how their happiness has been cast in the role of consumption, and a disposition to build social peace, their moderation of purchasing can result. After graphing their instincts to have, students can account for how much influences by materialism, commercialism, and industry are felt in their lives. Self-assessment of human participation in industry for mass production of goods illuminates the connection between consumerism and production issues.

TABLE 5.1   *Case example*

Peace Seeds Newsletter

Discovering Fair Trade

Developing countries deserve a fair price for their work. Fair trade involves a wide range of merchandise such as tea, bananas, and cotton goods. Coffee beans are a particularly well-known example.

Have you heard the expression "fair trade"? It refers to fair trade between developed countries and developing countries. For most of the junior writers, learning about a cafe in Hiroshima that offers fair trade goods was the first time they heard this expression.

To study this issue, we interviewed experts in the field and examined reports produced by NGOs. We also communicated, by email, with some Palestinian women who are creating embroidered goods.

Through this research, we discovered the fact that there are many children in Africa whose long hours of hard work enable us to eat the chocolate we consume daily in Japan. And there are other people growing coffee beans who cannot earn enough income despite their best efforts. These situations forced us to reflect on the gap between the rich and the poor.

However, compared to Europe, the idea of fair trade is not widely known in Japan. To promote this idea, we want to spread the word and raise awareness among the Japanese people. (Japanese teens in Hiroshima, 2008, para. 1). Provided by the *Chugoku Shimbun*.

Teachers expand student awareness of ways people have engaged in economics, or might do so, with a focus on fulfillment of their life needs. Learners consider the idea of paying everyone a *Basic Income* that would provide support for all basic living needs working people have (Twine, 1994). Information about how people exchanged goods and services, organized monetary systems, and participated in an industrial revolution provides a foundation for considering more equitable economic interactions. Additionally, teachers help students recognize unjust and unsustainable practices that have been occurring in the past century as a result of economic systems. During examination of their personal engagements in those systems, students can see the relationship of their economic actions with a lack of well-being in the world. As mentioned before, they can connect their consumption of goods to labor practices and worker compensation, as well as identify disparity of value placed on roles in economic systems. With data about the pay levels of employees in organizations, students discern values that differential compensation conveys, including labor wages and management salaries. In recognition of undervalued work that makes well-being of workers difficult, or impossible, students learn about how people have organized to change such situations. Studying the history of labor movements, violent responses to them, as well as changes that were outcomes of those movements reveals the problems that have resulted from economic injustice (Bigelow & Diamond, 1988). With awareness of that history and the supportive disposition of fairness in economic relationships, students may envision alternative models of economic interactions. While developing a sociological imagination, students can see "the double involvement of individuals and institutions: we create society at the same time we are created by it" (Giddens, 1982, p. 14). Through "visioning the possible," David Korten (2006, p. 103) thought of changes that would focus on needs of living, versus consumerist having:

> Systems of production and exchange would be localized to create a strong connection to place and community, thereby reducing the physical distance between home, employment, commerce, and entertainment. Income and ownership would be equitably distributed and locally rooted to ground political democracy securely on a base of economic democracy and to achieve a more equitable needs-oriented distribution of real wealth.

While identifying current transformation actions, students can recognize personal and collective efforts to develop a green economy through initiatives such as lifestyle changes, socially and environmentally responsible consumption, and corporate responsibility (Henderson, 2006; Reynolds, 2002; Utset, Villanueva, & Gonzalo, 1998). Identification of marketing techniques helps students recognize opportunities for cultural renewal—rejecting unhealthy habits that advertisements encourage (Herd, 1997). They can anticipate how wholesome development and leadership will be a worthwhile economic pursuit for themselves as well as for others (Wakhlu, 1999).

Political citizenship

Students learn about political systems and how people in different models of governance make changes without violence. There are examples worldwide of political and economic noncooperation during liberation efforts (Bartkowski, 2013). With mindfulness about the goal of peace for everyone, students learn past as well as current methods of civic participation. For development of that awareness, along with dispositions that support cooperation in contentious political contexts and communication skills that clarify perceptions, students participate in real as well as simulated conflict resolution (Stevahn et al., 2002). Within multiple contexts, beyond school and community systems of governance, students acquire skills along with awareness and supportive dispositions. Optimal cultivation of their capabilities results from teachers and other school participants who recognize the developmental stages of political skill-building. Analysis of citizenship education across nations confirmed the centrality of the teacher, specifically with regard to cultural beliefs that influence formal and informal instruction (Kerr, 2002).

As school citizens, students learn informally through interaction as well as formally through planned lessons about their role and rights in the education system and its surrounding society. Campus-wide problem-solving programs like discussion circles and conflict mediation are learning contexts that optimally facilitate student power in pursuit of peace. Educators who discern these "pockets of peace" strive for equity of student opportunities in school while they demonstrate and explain its governance systems (Carter, 2004b). Correspondingly, teachers facilitate students' analysis of conflicts within their school structure. After doing that, students consider strategies of peace-focused transformation that might be used for bringing about needed changes on their campus. The "exemplary practice" of a democratic education has involved decentering of school leadership to facilitate a community of decision makers on the campus, which includes students and their families (Levinson & Brantmeier, 2006, p. 339).

Discipline in school is a context for mindful citizenship of educators, along with students. Restorative discipline provides students an opportunity to communicate about systems and their experiences in them that can be improved (Adams, 2008). Discipline with a restoration orientation has a goal of creating and restoring supportive relationships that promote mutual understanding in a school. Those relationships include school members and people in the community with whom the students interact. The program Restore360 uses restorative Circles for building community while it addresses harmful actions. It also has a prevention effect in development of student skills and sense of community (Morningside Center for Teaching Social Responsibility, 2014).

School democracy includes student participation in governance that facilitates student explanation of their perceptions and desires (Cannon, 2011). A student council in campus government expresses the needs of its student body. The program Raising Student Voice and Participation has student summits where participants discuss their needs and hopes (National Association of Student Councils, 2015). In addition to a focusing on needs on campus, student governments can interact with and proactively address issues in their community. The PEACE Week (People Encouraging And Caring for Each other) that Mansfield High School Student Council conducted had two goals. One was inspiring a sense of selflessness and the other was fundraising for relief programs in their community (Mansfield Independent School District, 2014).

While thinking about conflict students face, teachers analyze problems on campus to recognize problem sources, such as causes of felt oppression that students and their families describe. For campus and community peace, teachers identify unequal opportunities in addition to under-representation in school organizations, curricula, and governance: structural conflicts that perpetuate real oppression (Kumashiro, 2001). In recognition of systemic problems, educators model for student-engaged citizenship. When a teacher professionally requests provision of equal learning opportunities for all members, the students see that peace-focused citizenship includes assertiveness and professional communication about problems. Students recognize that their political responsibilities as members of a democracy include deliberate discourse in the pursuit of justice through equality rights for those who lack them.

Mindful and Engaged Citizenship 115

As contexts for citizenship education, fairness and justice in school are informal curriculum (Callendar & Wright, 2000; Levinson, 2012). With mindfulness about their informal instruction as role models, teachers describe some of their political engagements during which they evidence the moral foundation of their decisions and activities. They may state, *I value fairness so I am working for a change of laws that will provide equal rights*. From that sharing, students learn how personal and cultural beliefs are catalysts of political action. Accordingly, they learn how value-based decisions have characterized political conflicts and caused divisions in response to conflict.

Citizenship education fairly includes knowledge of nonviolent political solutions to value conflicts. Inclusive curricula that feature examples of peaceful political accomplishments by people of different cultures, genders, faiths, and governance systems provide students with theoretical and behavioral models. Students need representational models of political problem solvers who represent different backgrounds, genders, and age groups (Stone, 2000). Consequently, children who actively participated in politics should not be overlooked in development of citizenship curriculum. As students look at the bravery of Ruby Bridges and many youth whose activities for civil rights were documented, they see that age does not preclude civic engagement (Welch, 2001). They learn in the history of Samantha Smith that children have an important role in peacemaking communication across "enemy" borders. With that knowledge they can ask: *How can I reach out to those who we need to understand? What can we do to meet their needs as well as ours?* Greater infusion of women's history, herstory, can help students see possibilities for reaching out to the "other" (Carter & Pickett, 2014; National Women's History Project, 2007).

Students also need to know of those who worked in different models of government for nonviolent change. Although the model of governance has certainly been worthwhile, peace development has occurred outside of democracy, and democracy has not always generated peaceful conflict transformation. Students need to know that people in every political model must be mindful of how interactions as citizens have ripple effects across the world. For that awareness, students learn about the political accomplishments of autocratic leaders such as Louis-Philippe, the King of the France, and Hussein bin Talal, the King of Jordan, as well as single-party leadership such as Mikhail Gorbachev, the General Secretary of the Communist Party of the Soviet Union (Howarth, 1961). While they examine leadership in democracy, the students see the challenges that presidents managed without the use of war as a response to international conflict (Krieger, 2005). While in office and afterward, the efforts of Presidents Oscar Arias Sanchez of Costa Rica and James Carter in the USA enable students to see how political problem solving is a life-long engagement (Canfield et al., 2005). Examining the life of President Nelson Mandela reveals the transformation that occurs through persistence as a nonviolent political activist and leader as well as the role of forgiveness in transformation of structural and personal conflicts. Mindfulness that sustains nonviolence during difficult times and a vision of peace have been crucial components of political citizenship. They are precursors of action in all contexts of conflict (Halpern, 2008). While cultivating student commitment to citizenship participation, teachers highlight the power of nonviolence in the past and the present for bringing about needed change (Adler, 2001; Kahne & Sporte, 2008). With the goal of peace, students evaluate government's response to current conflicts and they formulate alternative models, where needed, for bringing about change (The Peace Alliance, 2013). Table 5.2 suggests instruction about the response of international government to needs of children worldwide. Analysis of reasons for ratification by most other nations, and non-ratification by the USA, of the United Nations Convention on the Rights of the Child is an evaluation opportunity (Office of the High Commissioner for Human Rights, 2004).

TABLE 5.2 *Children's rights instruction*

Lesson Plan
Rights of the Child

Lesson Goal
Students will examine and respond to the rights of children that the United Nations Convention on the Rights of the Child articulates.

Exploration
Students brainstorm the meaning of rights and classify them by ownership: those of adults, children, and animals. The teacher presents information about rights that have become policy (American Civil Liberties Union, 2006). Students consider and discuss how rights for children that policy protects might contribute to peace.

Development
Students analyze the contents of the Convention on Rights of the Child (available at http://www2.ohchr.org/english/bodies/crc/docs/CRC.C.BFA.3-4.pdf).
Students compare the history of children's rights, with special attention to differences of those rights that have been influenced by political responses to identity characteristics, including gender, ethnicity, and nationality.

Expansion
Students examine impediments to fulfillment of children's rights in their community, before they plan and take action to raise awareness about those unfulfilled rights (Amnesty International, 2015).

Conclusion

With the foundation of awareness and stewardship, mindful and engaged citizenship occurs in multiple domains. The many opportunities for participatory citizenship range from near to distant locations. Dispositions that enable comprehensive citizenship are born of and shaped by observations, experience, reflection, and peace-focused vision. Observation and reflection begin with self-examination. With that awareness, students develop personal responsibility for their role in relationships. In cultivating their vision of peace, they picture contexts in which people and other forms of life thrive without violence as a response to conflicts they recognize and work to resolve. Through social, environmental, ethical, geographic, economic, and political engagements, students learn how they can hold the world, as well as their school, together. Their conscientious teachers model for them the enactment of mindful citizenship.

Instructional opportunities. Teach students about comprehensive citizenship, which expresses hope for peace. Build their mindfulness and awareness of how their own courage supports change processes for avoidance of harm. Affirm their stewardship at school and in their communities. Have them illustrate their citizenship actions and everyday stewardship for documenting and sharing their peace-oriented accomplishments.

Curricular applications

1 How can you facilitate student reflection through mindful awareness? Describe processes that might be used in your class and across your campus for enhancing intrapersonal skills, self-understanding, and stress reduction.
2 Create a lesson plan for student analysis and use of two metaphors: *the elephant in the room* that represents an evident but unaddressed conflict; and *a raging elephant* that is like an undisciplined mind. Give them opportunities for identification of past and present conflicts that use of these metaphors could describe. Also, consider fostering their use of those metaphors while they bring to your attention current conflicts that need attention.
3 Consider, and then describe, how teachers might model for students the following dispositions that support peace: mutuality,

concern, stewardship, service, involvement, courage, commitment, and patience. Which disposition seems the most challenging for modeling by teachers? Why do you think that?
4. How could a school convey to its members and the families of its students the four reasons for hope as described by Jane Goodall? How would you stimulate from your students their ideas about other reasons for hope?
5. In what ways could students apply the notion of ecological democracy, which gives voice to ecosystems that humans have been damaging? Describe applications of that notion in different types of lessons. Describe your thoughts about adaptation of that notion for environments beyond planet earth.
6. Develop a lesson for student quantification, by counting the sources, and analysis of what influences their desire for material things. Facilitate as part of the lesson their reflection on how consumption in their society relates to other domains of citizenship.

Resources For Transformative Citizenship Education

Ashoka's Youth Venture (www.youthventure.org/)
Campaign for Civic Mission of Schools (http://www.civicmissionofschools.org/)
Collaborative for Academic, Social and Emotional Learning (www.casel.org/)
The Dalai Lama Foundation (www.dalailamafoundation.org)
Declaration on a culture of peace and non-violence for the children of the world, 2001–2010. Resolution 53/25. Retrieved from http://www3.unesco.org/iycp/uk/uk_sum_decade.htm
The Earth Charter (http://www.earthcharterinaction.org/content/)
Good Character Company (http://www.goodcharacter.com/chron/citizenship.html)
Institute for Peace and Justice (www.ipj-ppj.org)
Mindfulness Awareness Research Center (www.marc.ucla.edu/)
National Women's History Project (www.nwhp.org)
Peace Pledge (www.pledgepeace.org/)
Rethinking Schools (www.rethinkingschools.org/)
Second Step (www.cfchildren.org/second-step.aspx)
Teachers Without Borders (www.teacherswithoutborders.org)

Teaching for Change (www.teachingforchange.org)
Teaching Tolerance (www.tolerance.org)
United Nations Children's Emergency Fund (www.unicef.org)
United Nations Educational, Scientific and Cultural Organization (1998, November).

Expansion

1 Reflect on your citizenship foundations. What are your thoughts about them as an informal and formal educator as well as a comprehensive citizen?
2 Describe your self-mediation. Explain how you can or have used it when you encounter conflicts that involve identity group differences.
3 Illustrate and caption your current and future enactments of citizenship, in every strand, that promote peace.
4 Analyze, with a minimum of three perspectives, a current structural conflict. Explain what needs it evidences and multiple ideas about how they might be met.
5 Describe all of the current strands of citizenship education that are evident in curriculum at your school. Include informal as well as formal education.
6 Critically evaluate all strands of citizenship education that are evident in curriculum at a school. In that process, answer the following question using each strand of citizenship, "Who has the power?" In other words, explain the implicit message about control in each strand of citizenship. Then, suggest how those power relations might change in the expansion of peace.

Appendix: Standards for Peace Education

Standards for students

Students of peace education exhibit the following developmentally appropriate knowledge, skills, and dispositions.

Knowledge

Self-Awareness

Evidence: Recognize own values, emotional tendencies, peace capabilities.

Contextual Awareness

Evidence: Knowledge of history and current needs of people in the community.

Multiculturalism

Evidence: Describe commonalities with and experiences of peoples having different cultural norms and histories.

Human Rights

Evidence: Identify the rights of children that were delineated by the UN and ratified by most nations.

History of Peace Accomplishments

Evidence: Analyze accomplishments of people, organizations, and societies.

Nonviolent Service
Evidence: Identify peace-service options in conscription, government, and nongovernmental agencies.

Peace Strategies
Evidence: Recognize the difference between negative and positive methods of peace.

Conflict Sources
Evidence: Identify roots of violence that have led to local and global conflicts.

Pro-active Communication
Evidence: Identify positively transformative communication techniques.

Methods of Nonviolent Conflict Resolution
Evidence: Describe appropriate methods for different situations.

Conflict Style
Evidence: Identify own conflict-response style and alternative methods for resolving disputes.

Democratic Processes
Evidence: Identify methods of democratic decision making.

Environmental Stewardship
Evidence: Explain rationale for ecological care of the physical environment.

Consumerism
Evidence: Explain reasons for socially and environmentally responsible consumerism.

Skills

Self-Concept Expression
Evidence: Express a balanced self-concept using affirmation for valuing, as well as critique for self-improvement.

Analysis of Communication

Evidence: Identify techniques including representation, bias, balance, multiple perspectives, and active listening skills.

Communication Enactment

Evidence: Use multiple-perspective, cross-cultural, and compassionate discourse.

Empathy

Evidence: Show understanding of and concern for the suffering of others, whether it was caused by oneself or by someone in one's own identity group.

Inclusion

Evidence: Choose to include in personal and group activities people with diverse social, intellectual, and physical characteristics.

Community Partnerships

Evidence: Collaborate with people and organizations that promote peace without harm.

Cooperation

Evidence: Demonstrate ability to cooperate with others who have different goals.

Analysis of Violence Sources

Evidence: Identify disrespect, discrimination, deprivation, power imbalance, and destruction; thereby recognizing intrapersonal, interpersonal, and structural causes.

Perspective Diversity

Evidence: Learn from and explain three or more perspectives in conflict analysis.

Legitimize Others

Evidence: Validate the point of view, narrative, and aspirations of an adversary—one with a different goal.

Engagement

Evidence: Demonstrate thoughts and actions for bringing about and building peace.

Accommodations

Evidence: Accept and adapt to diverse cultural and cognitive norms of other people.

Collective and Individual Responsibility

Evidence: Acknowledge and explain own group or self-contribution to conflict.

Positive Recognition

Evidence: Acknowledge all efforts and accomplishments of disputants in a conflict.

Envision Peace

Evidence: Develop and express visions of a peaceful presence and future.

Commitment

Evidence: Commit to work for a peaceful presence and future through nonviolent conflict transformation and resolution.

Adaptation

Evidence: Practice peace development within cultural contexts using culturally appropriate methods.

Environmental Stewardship

Evidence: Participate in ecological care of the physical environment.

Restoration

Evidence: Use culturally responsive methods for repairing damage after harm to humans or to nature.

Consumerism

Evidence: Identify or participate in socially and environmentally responsible consumerism.

Dispositions

Acceptance

Evidence: Display acceptance of oneself and of human diversity.

Mutuality

Evidence: Show identification with all humanity while recognizing distinct needs of different groups.

Respect

Evidence: Exhibit positive regard for others, regardless of their differences from oneself.

Concern

Evidence: Demonstrate a conscience that monitors activities for protection of life and its environment.

Empathy

Evidence: Show compassion for those who suffer and have needs to fulfill.

Service

Evidence: Demonstrate an interest in providing assistance to anyone, including people with diverse characteristics, when it is needed.

Optimism

Evidence: Show belief that peace can grow out of pro-active conflict resolution.

Involvement

Evidence: Realize personal and collective responsibility to bring about change by peaceful means where it is needed.

Courage

Evidence: Show willingness to disrupt or stop antecedents of, as well as existing, violence.

Commitment

Evidence: Demonstrate desire to work for a peaceful presence and future.

Patience
Evidence: Show ability to wait for completion of steps in a peace process.

Standards for teachers

In addition to educating students with the recommended peace-education standards for them, teachers of primary and secondary levels of schooling demonstrate the following skills:

1. Facilitate student construction, from their collective experiences and new information, their concepts of peace and positive processes for increasing it.
2. Integrate positive contact with, as well as information about, diverse cultures in the local region and afar to overcome ignorance, misinformation, and stereotypes.
3. Accommodate cultural norms of students, including their diverse learning styles.
4. Engage in cross-cultural communication with multicultural school participants, including families, thereby modeling acceptance, accommodation, and celebration of diversity through pluralism.
5. Demonstrate positive regard for all students, regardless of their misbehaviors, to convey unconditional care and respect for them as valuable people.
6. Use compassionate and equitable communication in dialogic facilitation of classroom management.
7. Train students through modeling of dispositions and skills that develop peace, including the practice of nonviolence before and during conflicts.
8. Create a nurturing "school-home" environment which nourishes and provides a safe place for communication about concerns related to violence.
9. Listen to families' ideas of how peace can be developed in the classroom and school, and then collaborate with them in the facilitation of their suggestions.
10. Use strategies that support peaceful interaction with the self and all people, including restorative practices in post-conflict situations.

11. Model action for peace development on and beyond the campus, thereby demonstrating a community norm of social justice and environmental stewardship.
12. Cultivate and support the student's responsibility for their own peaceful problem solving while you stay aware of, and responsive to, their needs.
13. Integrate across multiple subject areas information about past, present, as well as future peace developments and strategies.
14. Create and support venues for expressing current and future peace development.
15. Show appreciation for all student achievements in, and aspirations for, peace.
16. Attend to and teach ecological care of the physical environment, including sustainable use of its resources.
17. Teach about socially and environmentally responsible consumerism and the conflicts which result from exploitation of producers and laborers.
18. Teach about power relations in current events as well as history to help students recognize sources of structural violence.
19. Facilitate student examination of militarism and its impact on the social order.
20. Teach students to critically evaluate sources, perspectives, and evidence provided in information they have access to while enabling them to recognize the types of information they do not have, but need, to develop clear understanding of spoken and written presentations.
21. Enable students' discussions of controversy and unresolved problems locally and globally, thereby cultivating their intellectual and communicative skills for comprehending and analyzing conflicts.

Standards for teacher educators

Teacher educators use goals of peace development to identify competencies for student dispositions, knowledge, and skills to accomplish relevant field experiences and internships in students' courses.

1. Include peace education standards in course syllabi and content to clarify instructional goals.

2. Provide opportunities for pre-service teachers to identify, then examine, their awareness, views, and biases.
3. Legitimize diverse viewpoints and enable students to express their own to develop their civil courage and public voices.
4. Build teachers-in-training's self-respect along with positive regard for diverse others as they develop their peacebuilding knowledge, skills, and dispositions.
5. Study, model, and teach alternative positions before taking a stance on an issue.
6. Facilitate and use lateral, creative, and critical thinking processes.
7. Teach how to obtain information about, and then analyze, power relations that are evident in local to global interactions, including analysis of international relations as outcomes of economic systems and political domination, such as capitalism and imperialism.
8. Teach about how social structures and institutions that perpetuate systemic violence and societal conflicts such as poverty, racism, sexism, and homophobia.
9. Make oppression evident to students, and denounce it.
10. Teach about multiple aspects of democratic citizenship including social, environmental, economic, and political responsibilities for participation in a democracy.
11. Make clear the distinction between democracy and capitalism.
12. Illustrate how consumption practices and international policies affect human relations and the environment.
13. Develop the capacity to learn about and facilitate pro-active responses to conflicts, including contentious issues.
14. Develop tolerance for uncertainty with open processes, thereby allowing students to explore multiple ways of approaching tasks, including conflict resolution.
15. Encourage students to create social and environmental action projects in response to community, national, and global conflicts.
16. Provide examples of and model proactive responses to conflict (e.g., be able to understand/legitimate other points of view with which you don't agree; decallage, uncertainty).
17. Emphasize responsibility for peacebuilding and nonviolence in all settings by proactively addressing intrapersonal, interpersonal, and systemic problems.
18. Persistently address the unresolved learning issues of teacher candidates, including use of positive conflict management skills.

19 Recognize and affirm the use of peacebuilding and peacemaking strategies in the classes, field experiences, and internships of a teacher-training program.
20 Extend support for teacher development, within and beyond initial credential training, through individual as well as group reflection and research.
21 Document, evaluate, and professionally share the successes and challenges of peace-focused teacher education.
22 Revise teacher-training approaches in response to examination of their outcomes.

Standards for school administrators

School administrators practice the following peacemaking skills.

1 Model dispositions and skills that develop peace.
2 Engage in cross-cultural communication with multicultural school participants, including families, thereby modeling acceptance, accommodation, and celebration of diversity through pluralism.
3 Demonstratively value and recognize cooperation and mutual support of all school participants.
4 Use peaceful interaction with oneself and all people at the school, thereby reducing tension for the school participants.
5 Enact non-hegemonic leadership in which supremacy over, and domination of, others is not used to manage the conflicts at a school.
6 Use congenial and equitable problem solving—Theory Y.
7 Cultivate and support student, family, and school-staff responsibility for their own peaceful problem solving while staying aware of, and responsive to, their needs.
8 Express appreciation for all student achievements in, and aspirations for, peace.
9 Extend support for teacher development, within and beyond initial credential training, through individual as well as group reflection and research.
10 Encourage the use of the school as a site for community collaboration among parents, students, and all school staff.

11. Provide opportunities for peace education instruction of, and involvement by, families and other school partners including the school as a place for citizenship enactment.
12. Include peace maintenance and development as criteria for inclusion in evaluation of all school personnel.
13. Support initiatives in peace-oriented education by school members, including use and disposal of materials at school as well as curriculum and instruction.
14. Recognize by documenting peace-oriented outcomes of education when evaluating faculty and other school staff.
15. Emphasize nonviolence in all systems of, and interactions at, a school.

—2006, Revised 2013, Candice C. Carter

References

Adams, C. (2008). The talk it out solution. *Scholastic Administrator Magazine*. November/December. Retrieved from http://www2.scholastic.com/browse/article.jsp?id=3750554

Adams, D. (With Foundation for a Culture of Peace). (2005). *World Report on the Decade for a Culture of Peace*. Retrieved from http://decade-culture-of-peace.org/report/wrcpx.pdf

▶ Adler, S. (2001). An NCSS commitment: Educating students to be effective, participatory citizens. *The Social Studies Professional*, 163, May/June, 1–3.

Alaska Native Knowledge Network. (1998). *Alaska standards for culturally-responsive schools*. Anchorage, AK: Author. Retrieved from http://ankn.uaf.edu/publications/culturalstandards.pdf

Alleman, J., & Brophy, J. (1991). *Is curriculum integration a boon or a threat to social studies: Research Series No. 204* (ED337388). Washington, DC: Department of Education.

Alleman, J., & Brophy, J. (1994). Taking advantage of out-of-school opportunities for meaningful social studies learning. *The Social Studies*, 85(6), 262–267. doi:10.1080/00377996.1994.9956316

Alleman, J., Knighton, B., & Brophy, J. (2007). Social studies: Incorporating all children using community and cultural universals as the centerpiece. *Journal of Learning Disabilities*, 40(2), 166–173. doi: 10.1177/00222194070400020701

American Civil Liberties Union. (2006). *Rights matter: The story of the Bill of Rights*. Retrieved from http://www.rightsmatter.org/curriculum/index.html

Amnesty International. (2005). *Human rights for human dignity: A primer on economic, social and cultural rights*. Oxford, UK: Alden.

Amnesty International. (2007). A new look at equality: Teaching economic rights in our schools. *Fourth R*, 17(1), entire edition.

Amnesty International. (2015). *Youth in action*. Retrieved from http://www.amnestyusa.org/resources/students-and-youth

Amstutz, L. S., & Mullet, J. H. (2005). *The little book of restorative discipline for schools: Teaching responsibility; creating caring climates*. Intercourse, PA: Good Books.

Anderson, D., & Lubig, J. (2012). The missing link: Peer conferencing in civics education. *Social Studies*, 103(5), 201–205.

Andrzejewski, J., Pedersen, H., & Wicklund, F. (2009). Interspecies education for humans, animals, and the Earth. In J. Andrzejewski, M. Baltodano, & L. Symcox (eds), *Social justice, peace, and environmental education: Transformative standards* (pp. 136–158). New York: Routledge.

Apple, M. (1995). *Education and power* (2nd edition). New York, NY: Routledge.

Assembly of Alaska Native Educators. (1998). *Alaska standards for culturally responsive schools*. Retrieved from http://ankn.uaf.edu/publications/culturalstandards.pdf

Au, W. (2000). Teaching about the WTO and global issues. *Rethinking schools*, 14(3). Retrieved from http://www.rethinkingschools.org/restrict.asp?path=archive/14_03/wto143.shtml

Au, W., Bigelow, B., & Karp, S. (2007). *Rethinking our classrooms: Teaching for equity and justice* (Vol. 1). Milwaukee, WI: Rethinking Schools.

Avery, P. G., & Simmons, A. M. (2000). Civic life as conveyed in United States civics and history textbooks. *International Journal of Social Education*, 15(2), 105–130.

Bae, J. (2012). An intercultural peace mural project: Let's make a peaceful world hand in hand. *Art Education*, 65(1), 47–54.

Banks, J. (1997). Education for survival in a multicultural world. In M. E. Haas, & M. A. Laughlin (eds), *Meeting the standards: Social studies readings for K-6 educators* (pp. 231–232). Washington, DC: National Council for the Social Studies.

Banks, J. (2014). *An introduction to multicultural education* (5th edition). New York, NY: Pearson.

Banks, J. A. (2008). Diversity, group identity, and citizenship education in a global age. *Educational Researcher*, 37(3), 129–139.

Bar-On, D., & Adwan, S. (2006). The prime shared history project: Peace-building under fire. In Y. Iram, H. Wahrman, & Z. Gross (eds), *Educating toward a culture of peace* (pp. 309–323). Charlotte, NC: Information Age.

Bartkowski, M. J. (ed.). (2013). *Recovering nonviolent history: Civil resistance in liberation struggles* (pp. 299–317). London: Lynne Rienner.

Basile, C., White, C., & Robinson, S. (2000). *Awareness to citizenship: Environmental literacy for the elementary child*. New York, NY: University Press of America.

Bellah, R. N., Madsen, R., Sullivan, W. M., Swidler, A., & Tipton, S. M. (1991). *The good society*. New York, NY: Random House.

Bendik-Keymer, J. (2006). *The ecological life: Discovering citizenship and a sense of humanity*. Lanham, MD: Rowman & Littlefield.

Berdan, K., Boulton, I., Eidman-Aadahl, E., Fleming, J., Gardner, L., Rogers, I., & Solomon, A. (eds). (2006). *Writing for a change: Boosting literacy and learning through social action*. San Francisco, CA: Jossey-Bass.

Berry, T. (1984). The cosmology of peace. *Breakthrough*, 5(4), 1–4. Global Education Associates.

Bertling, J. (2013). Exercising the ecological imagination: Representing the future of place. *Art Education*, 66(1), 33–39.

Bible Study Tools. (2013). *Proverbs 29:18 (King James version)*. Author. Retrieved from http://www.biblestudytools.com/kjv/proverbs/29-18.html

Bigelow, B. (1993). The singing strike and the rebel students. *Teaching for Change*, Theme Songs for Social Justice. Winter 1993–1994, 3–7.

Bigelow, W. (2008). *A people's history for the classroom*. Williston, VT: Rethinking Schools.

Bigelow, W., & Diamond, N. (1988). *The power in our hands. A curriculum on the history of work and workers in the United States*. New York: Monthly Review.

Boulding, E. (1988a). *Building a global civic culture: Education for an interdependent world*. New York, NY: Teachers College Press.

Boulding, E. (1988b). Image and action in peace building. *Journal of Social Issues*, 44(2), 17–37. doi:10.1111/j.1540-4560.1988.tb02061.x

Boulding, E. (1992). Strategies for learning peace. In J. Lynch, C. Modgil, & S. Modgil (eds), *Cultural diversity and the schools* (pp. 205–215). London: Falmer.

Boulding, E. (2000). Envisioning the peaceable kingdom. In W. Wink (ed.), *Peace is the way: Writings on nonviolence from the fellowship of reconciliation* (Part 3, Spirit of peace, pp. 29–134). Maryknoll, NY: Orbis Books.

Boulding, E., & Boulding, K. (1995). *The future: Image and process.* Thousand Oaks, CA: Sage.

Bourdieu, P., & Passeron, J. C. (1990). *Reproduction in education, society and culture* (2nd edition). Thousand Oaks, CA: Sage.

Bowers, C. A. (1993). *Education, cultural myths, and the ecological crisis: Toward deep changes.* Albany, NY: State University of New York.

Bowers, C. A. (2001). *Educating for eco-justice and community.* Athens, GA: University of Georgia.

Boyle-Baise, M., & Zevin, Z. (2009). *Young citizens of the world: Teaching elementary social studies through civic engagement.* New York, NY: Routledge.

Brameld, T. (1956/2010). *Toward a reconstructed philosophy of education.* Hillsdale, IL: Dryden.

Brantmeier, E. J., Lin, J., & Miller, J. P. (eds). (2010). *Spirituality, religion, and peace education.* Charlotte, NC: Information Age.

Braungart, R. G., & Braungart, M. M. (1998). Youth violence, citizenship, and citizenship education in the United States. In M. W. Watts (ed.), *Cross-cultural perspectives on youth and violence* (pp. 213–251). Stamford, CT: JAI Press.

Brophy, J. (1990). Teaching social studies for understanding and higher-order applications. *The Elementary School Journal,* 90(4), 351–417.

Brophy, J., & Alleman, J. (2009). Meaningful social studies for elementary students. *Teachers and Teaching: Theory and Practice,* 15(3), 357–376. doi:10.1080/13540600903056700

Brown, D. F. (2011). Curriculum integration: Meaningful learning based on students' questions. *Middle Grades Research Journal,* 6(4), 193–206.

Bstan-'Dzin-Rgy. (2001). *Ethics for the new millennium: His Holiness the Dalai Lama.* New York, NY: Riverhead Books.

Burke, A., & Hawkins, K. (2012). Mindfulness in education: Wellness from the inside out. *Encounter,* 25(4), 36–40.

Butroyd, B. (2001). Secondary subject teaching and the development of pupil values. In C. Cullingford, & P. Oliver (eds), *The national curriculum and its effects* (pp. 79–101). Burlington, VT: Ashgate.

Butzow, C. M., & Butzow, J. W. (1999). *Exploring the environment through children's literature: An integrated approach*. Englewood, CO: Teacher Ideas Press.

California Department of Education. (1996). *Visual and performing arts framework for California Public Schools, Kindergarten through grade twelve*. Sacramento, CA: Author.

California Department of Education. (2008). *Health education content standards for California public schools: Kindergarten through grade twelve*. Retrieved from http://www.cde.ca.gov/be/st/ss/documents/healthstandmar08.pdf

California Department of Education. (2014). *California history/social science framework and standards*. Retrieved from http://score.rims.k12.ca.us/standards/framework/

Callendar, C., & Wright, C. (2000). Discipline and democracy: Race, gender, school sanctions and control. In M. Arnot, & J.-A. Dillabough (eds), *Challenging democracy: International perspectives on gender, education and citizenship* (pp. 216–237). New York, NY: Routledge.

Camicia, S. P., & Saavedra, C. M. (2009). A new childhood social studies curriculum for a new generation of citizenship. *International Journal of Children's Rights*, 17(3), 501–517. doi:10.1163/157181809X441362

Campbell, S. (1998). *A guide for training study circle facilitators*. Study Circles Resource Center. Retrieved from http://www.awcnet.org/documents/tools_studycirclefacilitatorsguide.pdf

Canfield, J., Hansen, M. V., Carter, C. C., Palomares, S., Williams, L. K., & Winch, B. L. (eds). (2005). *Chicken soup for the soul: Stories for a better world*. New York, NY: Simon & Schuster.

Cannon, S. G. (2011). *Think, care, act: Teaching for a peaceful future*. Charlotte, NC: Information Age.

Cardoso, O. J. (1997). The cheese for nobody. In P. Bush (ed.), *The voices of the turtle: An anthology of Cuban stories* (pp. 170–177). London: Quartet.

Carter, C. C. (2003). Prosocial music: Empowerment through aesthetic instruction. *Multicultural Perspectives*, 5(4), 38–40.

Carter, C. C. (2004a). Education for peace in Northern Ireland and the USA. *Theory and Research in Social Education*, 32(1), 24–38. doi:10.1080/00933104.2004.10473241

Carter, C. C. (2004b). Whither social studies? In pockets of peace at school. *Journal of Peace Education*, 1(1), 77–87.

Carter, C. C. (2005). Reaching out for the other. In J. Canfield, M. V. Hansen, C. C. Carter, S. Palomares, L. K. Williams, & B. L. Winch (eds), *Chicken soup for the soul: Stories for a better world* (pp. 326–329). New York, NY: Simon & Schuster.

Carter, C. C. (ed.). (2010a). *Conflict resolution and peace education: Transformations across disciplines.* New York, NY: Palgrave Macmillan.

Carter, C. C. (2010b). Restorative practices for reconstruction. In C. C. Carter, & R. Kumar (eds), *Peace philosophy in action* (pp. 163–184). New York, NY: Palgrave Macmillan.

Carter, C. C. (2012). Restorative practices as formal and informal education. *Journal of Peace Education,* 9(2), 1–15. doi:10.1080/17400201.2012.721092

Carter, C. C. (2013). Standards for peace education. In I. M. Harris, & M. L. Morrison (eds), *Peace education* (3rd edition). Jefferson, NC: McFarland.

Carter, C. C., & Kumar, R. (eds). (2010) *Peace philosophy in action* (pp. 141–159). New York: Palgrave Macmillan.

Carter, C. C., & Mason, D. (1997, March). *A review of the literature on the cognitive effects of curriculum integration.* Paper presented at the meeting of the American Educational Research Association, Chicago, IL.

Carter, C. C., & Pickett, L. (2014). *Youth literature for peace education.* New York, NY: Palgrave Macmillan.

Catterall, J. (2007). Enahancing peer conflict resolution skills through drama: An experimental case study. *Research in Drama Education,* 12(2), 163–178.

Cavanagh, T. (2009). Creating a new discourse of peace in schools: Restorative justice in education. *The Journal for Peace and Justice Studies,* 18(1–2), 62–85. doi:10.5840/peacejustice2009181/25

The Center for Contemplative Mind in Society. (2013). *The tree of contemplative practices.* Author. Retrieved from http://www.contemplativemind.org/practices/tree

Center for Nonviolent Communication. (2013). *Resources.* Author. Retrieved from https://www.cnvc.org/learn/resources

Chandler, P., & McKnight, D. (2009). The failure of social education in the United States: A critique of teaching the national story from White colourblind eyes. *Journal for Education Policy Studies,* 7(2), 217–248.

Chandler, P., & McKnight, D. (2012). Race and social studies. In W. B. Russell III (ed.), *Contemporary social studies: An essential reader* (pp. 215–242). Charlotte, NC: Information Age.

Charalambous, C., Charalambous, P., & Zemblas, M. (2013). Doing "leftist propaganda" or working towards peace? Moving Greek-Cypriot peace education struggles beyond local political complexities. *Journal of Peace Education*, 10(1), 67–87. doi:10.1080/1740 0201.2012.741522

Chittenden Central Supervisory Union. (2015). *Power standards: Designing 21st Century universal classrooms*. Retrieved at http://www.ccsuvt.org/curriculum-instruction-and-assessment/curriculum/power-standards

Christensen, L. (2003). *Reading, writing, and rising up: Teaching about social justice and the power of the written word*. Milwaukee, WI: Rethinking Schools.

Clark, D. (2010). Bloom's taxonomy of learning domains. *Big dog & little dog's performance justapostion*. Retrieved from http://www.nwlink.com/~donclark/hrd/bloom.html#affective

Cleary, L. M., & Peacock, T. D. (1998). *Collected wisdom: American Indian education*. Boston, MA: Allyn & Bacon.

Collaborative for Academic, Social and Emotional Learning. (2015). Federal policy. Retrieved from https://casel.squarespace.com/academic-social-and-emotional-https://casel.squarespace.com/academic-social-and-emotional-learning-act

Comer, J. P. (2004). *Leave no child behind: Preparing today's youth for tomorrow's world*. New Haven, CT: Yale University Press.

Constitutional Rights Foundation. (2013). Online lessons. *School violence*. Retrieved from http://www.crf-usa.org/school-violence/school-violence.html

Cornbleth, C. (2002). What constrains meaningful social studies teaching. *Social Education*, 66(3), 186–190.

Cortés, C. E. (2000). *The children are watching: How the media teach about diversity*. New York, NY: Teachers College Press.

Counts, G. S. (1932). *Dare the schools build a new social order*. New York, NY: John Day.

Cranton, P. (2002). Teaching for transformation. In J. M. Ross-Gordon (ed.), *Contemporary viewpoints for teaching adults effectively*. New Directions for Adult and Continuing Education, 93, 63–71. doi:10.1002/ace.50

Crawford, P. A. (2005). Primarily peaceful: Nurturing peace in the primary grades. *Early Childhood Education Journal*, 32(5), 321–328. doi:10.1007/s10643-004-1083-7

Crocco, M. S. (1998). Crafting a culturally responsive pedagogy in an age of educational standards. *Theory and Research in Social Education*, 26(1), 123–130. doi:10.1080/00933104.1998.10505839

Crocco, M. S. (2000). Women, citizenship, and the social studies. *The Educational Forum*, 65(1), 52–59.

Cruz, B. C., & Thornton, S. J. (2013). Teaching social studies to English language learners (2nd edition). In T. Erben, B. C. Cruz, & S. J. Thornton (Series eds), *Teaching English Language Learners across the Curriculum*. New York, NY: Routledge.

Curti, M. (1985). Reflections on the genesis and growth of peace history. *Peace and Change*, 11(1), 1–18. doi:10.1111/j.1468-0130.1985.tb00069.x

D'Ambrosio, U. (ed.). (2008). Peace, social justice and ethnomathematics. In B. Sriraman (ed.), *International perspectives on social justice in mathematics education* (pp. 37–50). Charlotte, NC: Information Age.

Dajani, M. (2006). Big dream/small hope. In Y. Iram, H. Wahrman, & Z. Gross (eds). *Educating toward a culture of peace* (pp. 39–53). Charlotte, NC: Information Age.

The Dalai Lama Foundation. (2006). *The missing peace curriculum*. Retrieved from http://www.dalailamafoundation.org/members/en/tmpp.jsp

Daly, H. E., & Farley, J. (2004). *Ecological economics: Principles and applications*. London: Island.

Danesh, H. B. (2006). Towards an integrative theory of peace education. *Journal of Peace Education*, 3(1), 55–78. doi:10.1080/17400200500532151

Danesh, H. B. (2008). Unity-based peace education. In M. Bajaj (ed.), *Encyclopedia of peace education*. Charlotte, NC: Information Age. Retrieved from http://www.tc.edu/centers/epe/entries.html

Darder, A. (2011). *A dissident voice: Essays on culture, pedagogy and power*. New York: Peter Lang.

Darling, L. F. (2002). The essential moral dimensions of citizenship education: What should we teach? *Journal of Educational Thought*, 36(3), 229–247.

de los Reyes, E., & P. Gozemba. (2002). *Pockets of hope. How students and teachers change the world*. Westport, CT: Bergin and Garvey.

de Matos, F. G. (2003). Applied peace linguistics. *Reading Today*, (October/November), 18.

DePaul, Savarimuthu V. (2010). Peace education in elementary teacher education of Tamilnadu. In C. C. Carter (ed.), *Peace philosophy in action* (pp. 141–159). New York: Palgrave Macmillan.

De Pauw, L. G. (1975). *Founding mothers: Women of America in the Revolutionary Era*. Boston, MA: Houghton Mifflin.

Dewey, J. (1897). My pedagogic creed. *School Journal*, 54(3), (January 16), 77–80. Retrieved from http://en.wikisource.org/wiki/My_Pedagogic_Creed

Diamond, L. (2000). *The courage for peace*. Berkeley, CA: Conari.

Diem, R. (1996). Using social studies as the catalyst for curriculum integration. *Social Education*, 60(2), 95–98.

Diller, J. V., & Moule, J. (2005). *Cultural competence: A primer for educators*. Belmont, CA: Wadsworth.

Donnison, D. (1995). The good city and its civic leaders. In C. Crouch, & Marquand (eds), *Reinventing collective action: From the global to the local* (pp. 88–102). Cambridge, MA: Blackwell.

Dresser, N. (1996). *Multicultural manners: New rules of etiquette for a changing society*. New York, NY: John Wiley and Sons.

Dryzek, J. S. (2005). *The politics of the earth: Environmental discourses* (2nd edition). Oxford, NY: Oxford University Press.

Duckworth, C. L., Allen, B., & Williams, T. T. (2012). What do students learn when we teach peace? A qualitative assessment of a theater peace program. *Journal of Peace Education*, 9(1), 81–99. doi:10.1080/17400201.2012.664548

Dumais, S. A. (2002). Cultural capital, gender, and school success: The role of habitus. *Sociology of Education*, 75(1), 44–68.

Earth and Peace Education Associates. (2013). EPE values: Ecological sustainability. Retrieved from http://www.globalepe.org/content.php?nid=15

Earth Charter Initiative. (2012). *The Earth Charter*. Retrieved from http://www.earthcharterinaction.org/content/pages/Read-the-Charter.html

Education for Peace International. (n.d.). *Education for peace: Training a civilization of peace*. Retrieved from http://efpinternational.org

Egan, K. (1992). *Imagination in teaching and learning: Ages 8 to 15*. New York, NY: Routledge.

Eisner, E. (1991). Art, music, and literature within social studies. In J. P. Shaver (ed.), *Handbook of research on social studies teaching and learning* (pp. 552–558). New York, NY: MacMillan.

Eisler, R. (2000). *Tomorrow's children: A blueprint for partnership education in the 21st Century*. Boulder, CO: Westview Press.

Eldridge, M. (1998). *Transforming experience: John Dewey's cultural instrumentalism*. Vanderbilt University Press.

Elias, M. J., & Arnold, H. (eds). (2006). *The educator's guide to emotional intelligence and academic achievement: Social-emotional learning in the classroom*. Thousand Oaks, CA: Corwin Press.

Elias, M. J., Zins, J. E., Graczyk, P. A., & Weissberg, R. P. (2003). Implementations, sustainability, and scaling up of social-emotional and academic innovations in public schools. *School Psychology Review*, 32(3), 303–319.

Emerson, K., Movius, H., & Merideth, R. (1999). Trouble in Tortuga! A role-playing simulation game for teaching environmental conflict resolution. Udall Center for Studies in Public Policy. Retrieved at http://udallcenter.arizona.edu/publications/epp/pdfs/1999_emerson.MERIDETH.etal_trouble.in.tortuga.pdf

Epstein, T. (2001). Racial identity and young people's perspectives on social education. *Theory into Practice*, 40(1), 42–47.

Ethridge, E. A., & Branscomb, K. R. (2009). Learning through action: Parallel learning processes in children and adults. *Teaching and Teacher Education*, 25(3), 400–408. doi:10.1016/j.tate.2008.09.004

Etzioni, A. (1991). Social science as a multicultural canon. *Society*, 29(1), 14–18. Retrieved June from http://www.gwu.edu/~ccps/etzioni/A218.pdf

Evans, R. W., & Saxe, D. W. (eds). (1996). *Handbook on teaching social issues*. Washington, DC: National Council for the Social Studies.

Finley, L. L. (2011). *Building a peaceful society: Creative integration of peace education*. Charlotte, NC: Information Age.

Fisk, L. (2000). Shaping visionaries: Nurturing peace through education. In L. Fisk, & J. Schellenberg (eds), *Patterns of conflict, paths to peace* (pp. 159–193). Orchard Park, NY: Broadview.

Fitchett, P. G., & Heafner, T. L. (2012). Culturally responsive social studies teaching: Models of theory into practice. In W. B. Russell III (ed.), *Contemporary social studies: An essential reader* (pp. 195–214). Charlotte, NC: Information Age.

Florida Department of Education. (2008). *Next generation sunshine state standards*. Retrieved from http://www.cpalms.org/Standards/FLStandardSearch.aspx

Fogarty, R., & Stoehr, J. (1991). *Integrating curricula with multiple intelligences: Teams, themes, and threads*. Palatine, IL: Skylight.

Foster, J. B. (2009). *The ecological revolution: Making peace with the planet*. New York, NY: Monthly Review Press.

Four Arrows (aka Jacobs, D. T.). (2010). Indigenous spirituality as a source for peaceful relations. In E. J. Brantmeier, J. Lin, & J. P. Miller (eds), *Spirituality, religion, and peace education* (pp. 133–146). Charlotte, NC: Information Age.

Four Arrows, & Mann, B. (2013). *Teaching truly: A curriculum to indigenize mainstream education*. New York: Peter Lang.

Freire, P. (1973). *Education for critical consciousness*. New York: Seabury.

Freire, P. (1998). *Pedagogy of freedom: Ethics, democracy, and civic courage*. (P. Clarke, trans.). Lanham, MD: Rowman & Littlefield.

Friedrich, P. (2007). English for peace: Toward a framework for Peace Sociolinguistics. *World Englishes*, 26(1), 72–83.

Fritzsche, K. P. (2006). Tolerance education and human rights education in times of fear: A comparative perspective. In Y. Iram, H. Wahrman, & Z. Gross (eds), *Educating toward a culture of peace* (pp. 297–307). Charlotte, NC: Information Age.

Fromm, E. (1979). *To have or to be?* London: Abacus.

Galinsky, E., & Salmond, K. (2002). *Ask the children: Youth and violence*. Denver, CO: The Colorado Trust.

Galtung, J. (2004). *Transcend and transform: An introduction to conflict work*. Boulder, CO: Paradigm.

Galtung, J., & Udayakumar, S. P. (2013). *More than a curriculum: Education for peace and development*. Charlotte, NC: Information Age.

Gardner, H. (1993). *Frames of mind: The theory of multiple intelligences*. New York, NY: Basic Books.

Gay, G. (2000). Culturally responsive teaching: Theory, research and practice. In J. A. Banks (Series ed.), *Multicultural Education Series*. New York, NY: Teachers College.

Gernstein, L. H., & Moescheberger, S. L. (2003). Building cultures of peace: An urgent task for counseling professionals. *Journal of Counseling and Development*, 81, 115–119.

Ghaderi, M. (2011). Peace-based curriculum based on the theories of difference and similarity. *Procedia Social and Behavioral Sciences*, 15, 3430–3440. doi:10.1016/j.sbspro.2011.04.314

Giddens, A. (1982). *Sociology: A brief, but critical, introduction*. London: Macmillan.

Gilbert, J. N., & Orlick, T. (1996). Evaluation of a life skills program with grade two children. *Elementary School Guidance and Counseling*, 31(2). doi:00135976.

Giroux, H. A. (1988). *Schooling and the struggle for public life: Critical pedagogy in the modern age*. Minneapolis, MN: University of Minnesota.

Glass, K. (2011, April). *Differentiated tools, strategies, and assessments for social studies, writing, reading and science classrooms*. Retrieved from http://www.sde.idaho.gov/site/title_one/conference11/pres/Idaho%20DI%202011%20PPt%20Kathy%20Glass.pdf

Global Exchange. (2008). *Fair trade holiday caroling*. Retrieved from http://youtu.be/gqAx6AfJB68

Global Exchange. (2014). *What about peace?* Retrieved from http://www.globalexchange.org/peace/campaigns/whataboutpeace

Global Network Against Weapons and Nuclear Power in Space. (2008). *Space Alert, 20* Summer/Fall. Retrieved from http://www.space4peace.org/

Global Network Against Weapons and Nuclear Power in Space. (2013). *Space Preservation Act of 2005*. Retrieved from http://www.space4peace.org/articles/kucinich_bill.htm

Goel, L., Johnson, N., Junglas, I., & Blake, I. (2010). Situated learning: Conceptualization and measurement. *Decision Sciences Journal of Innovative Education*, 8(1), 215–240. doi:10.1111/j.1540-4609.2009.00252.x

Goldberg, T., & Ron, Y. (2014). "Look, each side says something different": The impact of competing history teaching approaches on Jewish and Arab adolescents' discussion of the Jewish-Arab conflict. *Journal of Peace Education*, 11(1), 1–29. doi:10.1080/17400201.2013.777897

Golston, S. (2010). The revised NCSS Standards: Ideas for the classroom teacher. *Social Education*, 74(4), 210–216.

Gomes de Matos, F. (2002). Teaching vocabulary for peace education. *ESL Magazine*, 5(4), 22–23.

Goodall, J. (2005). Hope for peace. In D. Krieger, & C. Ong. (eds), *Hold hope: Wage peace: Inspiring individuals to take action for a better world* (pp. 7–13). Santa Barbara, CA: Capra.

Gottlieb, R. (2002). Linking movements and constructing a new vision: Environmental justice and community food security. In B. A. Minteer, & B. P. Taylor (eds), *Democracy and the claims of nature: Critical perspectives for a new century* (pp. 321–334). Lanham, MD: Rowman & Littlefield.

Greene, M. (1995). *Releasing the imagination: Essays on education, the arts, and social change*. San Francisco, CA: Jossey-Bass.

Grice, J. (2011). Curriculum integration in Ontario high schools. *Pathways: The Ontario Journal of Outdoor Education*, 24(1), 4–8. Retrieved from http://www.coeo.org/images/stories/Digital%20 Pathways/Pathways_24_1.pdf

Gross, F. E., Morton, P., & Poliner, R. A. (1993). *The power of numbers: A teacher's guide to mathematics in a social studies context*. Cambridge, MA: Educators for Social Responsibility.

Haavelsrud, M., & Stenberg, O. (2012). Analyzing peace pedagogies. *Journal of Peace Education*, 9(1), 65–80. doi:10.1080/17400201.2012.657617

Hadley, M. L. (ed.). (2001). *The spiritual roots of restorative justice*. Albany, NY: State University of New York Press.

Hague Appeal for Peace. (2000). *The Hague agenda for peace and justice in the 21st century*. Retrieved from http://www.haguepeace.org/resources/HagueAgendaPeace+Justice4The21stCentury.pdf

Hague Appeal for Peace. (2004). *The Tirana call for peace education*. Retrieved from http://www.haguepeace.org/files/TheTiranaCallforPeaceEducation.pdf

Hahn, C. L. (2012). Becoming political: One woman's story. In S. Totten, & J. E. Pedersen (eds), *Researching and teaching social issues: The personal stories and pedagogical efforts of professors of education* (pp. 67–83). Charlotte, NC: Information Age.

Halpern, C. (2008). *Making waves and riding the currents: Activism and the practice of wisdom*. San Francisco, CA: Berrett-Koehler.

Harris, I. (2008). History of peace education. In M. Bajaj (ed.), *Encyclopedia of peace education*. Charlotte, NC: Information Age. Retrieved from http://www.tc.edu/centers/epe/entries.html

Harris, I. (ed.). (2013). *Peace education from the grassroots*. Charlotte, NC: Information Age.

Harris, I. M., & Morrison, M. L. (2013). *Peace education* (3rd edition). Jefferson, NC: McFarland.

Harste, J. (2000). Six points of departure. In B. Berghoff, K. A. Egawa, Harste, J. C., & B. T. Hoonan (eds), *Beyond reading and writing: Inquiry, curriculum, and multiple ways of knowing* (pp. 1–16). Urbana, IL: National Council of Teachers of English.

Hart, S. (2004). Creating a culture of peace with nonviolent communication. In R. Eisler, & R. Miller (eds), *Educating for a culture of peace* (pp. 113–125). Portsmouth, NH: Heinemann.

Hart, S., & Hodson, V. K. (2004). *The compassionate classroom: Relationship based teaching and learning*. Encinitas, CA: PuddleDancer Press.

Hart, T. (2004). Opening the contemplative mind in the classroom. *Journal of Transformative Education*, 2(1), 28–46. doi:10.1177/1541344603259311

Heafner, T. L. (2008). What does it mean to be a citizen: Defining social studies in the age of marginalization and globalization. *Journal of Curriculum and Instruction*, 2(1), 1–5. Retrieved from www.joci.ecu.edu/index.php/JoCI/article/view/8/10

Heath, D. H. (1994). *Schools of hope: Developing mind and character in today's youth*. San Francisco, CA: Jossey-Bass.

Helmsing, M. (2014). Virtuous subjects: A critical analysis of affective substance of social studies education. *Theory & Research in Social Education*, 42(1), 127–140.

Henderson, H. (2006). *Ethical markets: Growing the green economy*. White River Junction, VT: Chelsea Green.

Herd, D. A. (1997). The politics of representation: Marketing alcohol through rap music. In P. Sulkunen, J. Holmwood, H. Radner, & G. Schulze (eds), *Constructing the new consumer society* (pp. 134–151). New York, NY: St. Martin's Press.

Hester, C. (n.d). Lowering the affective filter. *Slideshare*. Retrieved from http://www.slideshare.net/caseyhester/lowering-the-affective-filter

Hicks, D. (2004). How can futures studies contribute to peace education. *Journal of Peace Education*, 1(2), 165–178.

Hill, C., Herndon, A. A., & Karpinska, Z. (2006). Contemplative practices: Educating for peace and tolerance. *Teachers College Record*, 108(9), 1723–1732.

Hoffman, G. K. (2008). Lesson plans for a course in compassionate listening. In G. K. Hoffman, C. Monroe, & L. Green (eds), *Compassionate listening: An exploratory sourcebook about conflict transformation* (pp. 15–24). Retrieved from http://www.newconversations.net/pdf/compassionate_listening.pdf

hooks, b. (2003). *Teaching community: A pedagogy of hope.* New York, NY: Routledge.

Hopkins, B. (2004). *Just schools: A whole school approach to restorative justice.* London: Jessica Kingsley.

Howarth, T. E. B. (1961). *Citizen-king: The life of Louis-Philippe, King of the French.* London: Eyre & Spottiswoode.

Human Rights Education Associates. (2005–2007). *World programme for human rights education: First phase (2005–2007).* Retrieved from http://www.hrea.org/world-programme/

Hursh, D. W., & Ross, E. W. (2000). *Democratic social education: Social studies for social change.* New York, NY: Falmer Press.

Hutchinson, F. P. (1996). *Educating beyond violent futures.* New York, NY: Routledge.

Hutchinson, F. P. (2002). *Towards the non-violent transformation of conflict: Working to transcend natural assumptions about violence and war.* July 2002. Paper presented at the Conference of the International Peace Research Association, Kyung Hee University, Suwon, South Korea.

Hutchinson, F. P., & Herborn, P. J. (2012). Landscapes for peace: A case study of active learning about urban environments and the future. *Futures,* 44(1), 24–35. doi:10.1016/j.futures.2011.08.004

Hyland, T. (2014). Mindfulness-based interventions and the affective domain of education. *Educational Studies,* 40(3), 277–291. doi:10.1080/03055698.2014.889596

Ikeda, D. (2005). Making hope. In D. Krieger, & C. Ong (eds), *Hold hope: Wage peace: Inspiring individuals to take action for a better world* (pp. 19–22). Santa Barbara, CA: Capra.

Ikeda, D. (2014). *Value creation for global change: Building resilient and sustainable societies.* Tokyo, Japan: Soka Gakkai International.

International Cities of Peace. (2012). *A vision for global community: Act local, connect global.* Retrieved from http://www.internationalcitiesofpeace.org/

International Network for Education in Emergencies. (2012). *Interview with Mary Kangethe on the Kenyan Ministry of Education's work on education and peace.* Author. December, 20. Retrieved from http://www.ineesite.org/en/blog/interview-with-mary-kangethe-on-the-kenyan-ministry-of-educations-work-on-e

Iram, Y., Wahrman, H., & Gross, Z. (eds). (2006). *Educating toward a culture of peace*. Charlotte, NC: Information Age.

Japanese teens in Hiroshima. (October 8, 2008). Discovering fair trade. *Peace Seeds Newsletter. Chugoku Shimbun, 17*, October. Retrieved from http://www.hiroshimapeacemedia.jp/hiroshima-koku/en/backnumber/index_special.html

Johnson, D. W., & Johnson, R. T. (1995). Teaching students to be peacemakers: Results of five years of research. *Peace and Conflict: Journal of Peace Psychology, 1*(4), 417–438. doi:10.1207/s15327949pac0104_8

Jones, V. (2007). A license to be human: An interview with Van Jones. In B. Lopez (ed.), *The future of nature: Writing on a human ecology from Orion Magazine* (pp. 53–61). Minneapolis, MN: Milkweed.

Kahne, J. E., & Sporte, S. (2008). Developing citizens: The impact of civic learning opportunities on students' commitment to civic participation. *American Educational Research Journal, 45*(3), 738–766.

Kant, I. (2003). *Observations on the feeling of the beautiful and the sublime* (J. T. Goldthwaite, trans.). Berkeley, CA: University of California Press.

Keating, J. (2013). The politics of space junk. *Articles*. Global Network against Weapons and Nuclear Power in Space. Retrieved from http://www.space4peace.org/articles/politics_of_space_junk.htm

Keen, S. (1986). *Faces of the enemy. Reflections of the hostile imagination*. New York, NY: Harper and Row.

Kendall, C. (September 23, 2008). A new law of nature: Ecuador next week votes on giving legal rights to rivers, forests and air. *The Guardian*, p. 8. Retrieved from http://www.guardian.co.uk/environment/2008/sep/24/equador.conservationhttp://www.guardian.co.uk/environment/2008/sep/24/equador.conservation

Kerr, D. (2002). Citizenship education: An international comparison across sixteen countries. *International Journal of Social Education, 17*(1), 1–15.

Kessler, R. (2005). Education for integrity, connection, compassion, and character. In R. Eisler, & R. Miller (eds), *Educating for a culture of peace* (pp. 57–79). Portsmouth, NH: Heinemann.

Kids for Peace. (2012). *Peace pledge*. Retrieved from http://kidsforpeaceglobal.org/

Kimura, T. (2009). The cosmology of peace and father Thomas Berry's great work. *The Japanese Journal of American Studies, 20*, 175–192. Retrieved from http://sv121.wadax.ne.jp/~jaas-gr-jp/jjas/PDF/2009/10_175-192.pdf

Kincheloe, J. L. (2001). Goin' home to the armadillo: Making sense of Texas educational standards. In R. A. Horn, & J. L. Kincheloe (eds), *American standards: Quality education in a complex world, the Texas case* (pp. 3–44). New York, NY: Peter Lang.

Kincheloe, J. L. (2005). *Critical pedagogy primer.* New York: Peter Lang.

King, M. L. Jr. (1963). Letter from a Birmingham jail. In M. L. King Jr. *Why we can't wait* (pp. 64–84). New York: Harper and Row.

Kleingeld, P. (1999). Kant, history, and the idea of moral development. *History of Philosophy Quarterly,* 16(1), 59–80. Retrieved from http://philosophy.eldoc.ub.rug.nl/FILES/root/1999/KantHistory/Kant_History_idea.pdf

Konidari, V., & Abernot, Y. (2008). The way classroom functions: Another hidden curriculum to be explored. *International Journal of Human and Social Sciences,* 3(1), 1–7.

Korn-Bursztyn , C. (ed.). (2012). *Young children and the arts: Nurturing imagination and creativity.* Charlotte, NC: Information Age.

Korten, D. (2006). The great turning. In R. Cavoukian, & S. Olfman (eds), *Child honoring: How to turn this world around* (pp. 95–103). London: Praeger.

Korty, C. (2002). Getting into the act: Interviews with six playwrights of participation theater. *Stage of the Art,* 15(1), 17–23.

Kramer, W. R. (2011). Colonizing Mars: An opportunity for reconsidering bioethical standards and obligations to future generations. *Futures,* 43(5), 545–551. doi:10.1016/j.futures.2011.02.006

Kreisberg, S. (1992). *Transforming power: Domination, empowerment, and education.* Albany, NY: State University of New York.

Krieger, D. (2005). The challenge of peace. In D. Krieger, & C. Ong (eds), *Hold hope: Wage Peace: Inspiring individuals to take action for a better world* (pp. 55–60). Santa Barbara, CA: Capra.

Kumashiro, K. (2001). "Posts" perspectives on anti-oppressive education in social studies, English, mathematics and science classrooms. *Educational Researcher,* 30(3), 3–12.

Lappin, R. (2009). Peacebuilding and the promise of transdisciplinarity. *International Journal on World Peace,* 26(3), 69–76.

Larson, C. L., & Ovando, C. J. (2001). *The color of bureaucracy: The politics of equity in multicultural school communities.* Belmont, CA: Wadsworth.

Lederach, J. P. (2003). *The little book of conflict transformation.* Intercourse, PA: Good Books.

Lee, N. P. (2013). Engaging the pink elephant in the room: Investigating race and racism through art education. *Studies in Art Education*, 54(2), 141–157.

Lemerise, E. A., & Arsenio, W. F. (2000). An integrated model of emotion processes and cognition in social information processing. *Child Development*, 71(1), 107–118.

Levin, T., & Nevo, Y. (2009). Exploring teachers' views on learning and teaching in the context of a trans-disciplinary curriculum. *Journal of Curriculum Studies*, 41(4), 439–465. doi:10.1080/00220270802210453

Levinson, B. A. U., & Brantmeier, E. J. (2006). Secondary schools and communities of practice for democratic civic education: Challenges of authority and authenticity. *Theory and Research in Social Education*, 34(3), 324–346.

Levinson, M. (2012). *No citizen left behind*. Cambridge, MA: Harvard University.

Lewis, B. (1998). *The kid's guide to social action: How to solve the social problems you choose-and turn creative thinking into positive action* (2nd edition). Minneapolis, MN: Free Spirit.

Lieber, C. M. (2003). The building blocks of conflict resolution education: Direct instruction, adult modeling, and core practices. In T. S. Jones, & R. Compton (eds), *Kids working it out: Stories and strategies for making peace in our schools* (pp. 35–59). San Francisco, CA: Jossey-Bass.

Lin, J. (2006). *Love, peace and wisdom in education: Vision for education in the 21st Century*. Lanham, MD: Rowman and Littlefield.

Lin, J., & Oxford, R. L. (2011). *Transformative eco-education for human and planetary survival*. Charlotte, NC: Information Age.

Linklater, A. (1998). Cosmopolitan citizenship. *Citizenship Studies*, 2(1), 23–41. doi:1080/13621029808420668

Lintner, T. (ed.). (2012). *Integrative strategies for the k-12 social studies classroom*. Charlotte, NC: Information Age.

Lintner, T., & Schweder, W. (eds). (2011). *Practical strategies for teaching k-12 social studies in inclusive classrooms*. Charlotte, NC: Information Age.

Lonberger, R., & Harrison, J. (2008). *Links to literature: Teaching tools to enhance literacy, character and social skills*. Cambridge, MA: Educators for Social Responsibility.

Lovejoy, N. (2007). SBHS students learn how to use conflict resolution in daily life. Schools. *Hollister Free Lance* p.1. May, 2. Retrieved from http://www.sanbenitocountytoday.com/news/schools/sbhs-students-learn-how-to-use-conflict-resolution-in-daily/image_5497cf1f-b853-506c-a15b-47107da58928.html

Lynn, E. H. (2008). *Stirring the head, heart, and soul: Redefining curriculum, instruction, and concept-based learning* (3rd edition). Thousand Oaks, CA: Corwin.

MacGinty, R. (2008). Indigenous peace-making versus the liberal peace. *Cooperation and Conflict*, 43(2), 139–163. doi:10.1177/0010836708089080

MacPhee, D. A., & Whitecotton, E. J. (2011). Bringing the social back to social studies: Literacy strategies as tools for understanding history. *The Social Studies*, 102(6), 263–267. doi:10.1080/00377996.2011.571300

Maebuta, J. (2011). Technical and vocational education and training in peace education: Solomon Islands. *Journal of Peace Education*, 8(2), 157–176. doi:10.1080/17400201.2011.589253

Maio, M. (2007). *Dramatic performances that demonstrate peace*. San Benito High School.

Mansfield Independent School District. (2014). *Mansfield High School Student Council's PEACE Week named Top 10 Project in the state*. Retrieved from http://www.mansfieldisd.org/page.cfm?p=4531&newsid=64#.VEoOuBaGq_w

Marri, A. R., Crocco, M. S., Shuttleworth, J., Gaudelli, W., & Grolnick, M. (2012). Analyzing social issues related to teaching about the federal budget, federal debt, and budget deficit in fifty state high school social studies standards. *Social Studies*, 103(4), 133–139.

Marshall, H. (2011). Instrumentalism, ideals and imaginaries: Theorising the contested space of global citizenship education in schools. *Globalisation, Societies and Education*, 9(3–4), 411–426. doi:10.1080/14767724.2011.605325

Mathis, J. B. (2001). Respond to stories with stories: Teachers discuss multicultural children's literature. *The Social Studies*, 92(4), 155–160. doi:10.1080/00377990109603995

Maxwell, A.-M., Enslin, P., & Maxwell, T. (2004). Educating for peace in the midst of violence: A South African experience. *Journal of Peace Education*, 1(1), 103–121. doi:10.1080/1740020032000178339

McGlynn, C., Niens, U., Cairns, E., & Hewstone, M. (2004). Moving out of conflict: The contribution of integrated schools in Northern Ireland to identity, attitudes, forgiveness and reconciliation. *Journal of Peace Education*, 1(2), 147–163. doi:10.1080/1740020042000253712

McLaren, P. (2003). *Life in schools: An introduction to critical pedagogy in the foundations of education* (4th edition). New York: Allyn & Bacon.

Meidl, T., & Meidl, C. (2011). Curriculum integration and adaptation: Individualizing pedagogy for linguistically and culturally diverse students. *Current Issues in Education*, 14(1). Retrieved on April 20, 2013, from http://cie.asu.edu/ojs/index.php/cieatasu/article/view/579

Mengual, G. F. (2008). Montgomery County (Md.) schools enlist Hispanic parent to improve student success. *Everyday Democracy*. February, 15. Retrieved from http://www.everyday-democracy.org/en/Article.694.aspx

Merchant, C. (2010). *Ecological revolutions: Nature, gender, and science in New England* (2nd edition). Chapel Hill, NC: University of North Carolina Press.

Merryfield, M. M., & Remy, R. C. (eds). (1995). *Teaching about international conflict and peace*. Albany, NY: State University of New York.

Mikkelson, P. (2008). I'll listen. *Journal of Stellar Peacemaking*, 3(2). Retrieved from http://74.127.11.121/peacejournal/volume_index/8/v3n2a4.html

Miller, J. P. (2010). Educating for wisdom. In E. J. Brantmeier, J. Lin, & J. P. Miller (eds), *Spirituality, religion, and peace education*, (pp. 261–275). Charlotte, NC: Information Age.

Miller, M. (2001). Teaching and learning in the affective domain. In M. Orey (ed.), *Emerging perspectives on learning, teaching and technology*. Retrieved from http://projects.coe.uga.edu/epltt/index.php?title=Teaching_and_Learning_in_Affective_Domain

Miller, M. (2006). Educating a culture of peace. In R. Cavoukian, & S. Olfman (eds), *Child honouring: How to turn this world around* (pp. 62–66). Westport, CT: Praeger.

Miller, R. (1990). *What are schools for: Holistic education in American culture*. Brandon, VT: Holistic Education.

Mills, R. K. (1997). Social studies and the spiritual nature of civic behavior. *Education*, 118(1), 59–62.

Mindfulness Awareness Research Center. (2008). *MAPs in education*. Retrieved from http://www.marc.ucla.edu/body.cfm?id=17&oTopID=17

Minteer, B. A., & Taylor, B. P. (eds). (2002). *Democracy and the claims of nature: Critical perspectives for a new century*. Lanham, MD: Rowman & Littlefield.

Mirk, P. (2013). Respect, compassion, and fairness in schools. *Whole Child Education*. February, 26. Retrieved from http://www.wholechildeducation.org/blog/respect-compassion-and-fairness-in-schools

Mische, P., & Harris, I. (2012). Environmental peacemaking, peacekeeping, and peacebuilding. In M. Bajaj (ed.), *Encyclopedia of peace education*. Charlotte, NC: Information Age. Retrieved from http://www.tc.edu/centers/epe/entries.html

Misco, T., Patterson, N., & Doppen, F. (2011). Policy in the way of practice: How assessment legislation is affecting social studies curriculum and instruction in Ohio. *International Journal of Education Policy and Leadership*, 6(7), 1–12.

Moaz, I. (2002). Conceptual mapping and evaluation of peace education programs: The case of education for coexistence through intergroup encounters between Jews and Arabs in Israel. In G. Salomon, & B. Nevo (eds), *Peace education: The concepts, principles, and practices around the world* (pp. 259–269). Mahwah, NJ: Lawrence Erlbaum.

Mobjörk, M. (2010). Consulting versus participatory transdisciplinarity: A refined classification of transdisciplinary research. *Futures*, 42(8), 866–873. doi:10.1016/j.futures.2010.03.003

Montessori, M. (1972). *Education and peace* (Helen R. Lane, trans.). Chicago: Regnery.

Montessori, M. (1992). *Education and peace* (Helen R. Lane, trans.). Oxford, England: Clio Press.

Morgan, B., & Vandrick, S. (2009). Imagining a peace curriculum: What second-language education brings to the table. *Peace & Change*, 34(4), 510–532. doi:10.1111/j.1468-0130.2009.00598.x

Morningside Center for Teaching Social Responsibility. (2014). *Restore360*. Retrieved from http://www.morningsidecenter.org/node/760/

Mucklow, N. (2009). *The sensory team handbook: A hands-on tool to help young people make sense of their senses and take charge of their sensory processing* (2nd edition). Kingston, Ontario: Michael Grass House.

Muller, R. (2012). From apathy to activism: Civic-mindedness, critical pedagogy, and the sociological imagination. *Theory in Action*, 5(2), 51–69. doi:10.3798/tia.1937-0237.12013

Murphy, G., & National Public Telecomputing Network. (2012). *The Constitution of the Iroquois Nations: The Great Binding Law, Gayanashagowa*. Retrieved from http://www.indigenouspeople.net/iroqcon.htm

Mustafa, J. (2011). Proposing a model for integration of social issues in school curriculum. *International Journal of Academic Research*, 3(1), 925–931.

Myles, B. S., Trautman, M. L., & Schelvan, R. L. (2004). *The hidden curriculum: Practical solutions for understanding unstated rules in social situations*. Shawnee Mission, KS: Autism Asperger Publishing.

Nabhan, G. P. (2007). Listening to the other: Can a sense of place help the peace-making process. In B. Lopez (ed.), *The future of nature: Writing on a human ecology from Orion Magazine* (pp. 341–352). Minneapolis, MN: Milkweed.

Nabudere, D. W. (2012). *Afrikology and transdisciplinarity: A restorative epistemology*. Pretoria: Africa Institute of South Africa.

Nagel, G. K. (1998). *The Tao of teaching: The ageless wisdom of Taoism and the art of teaching*. New York, NY: Plume.

Nagler, M. N. (2004). *The search for a nonviolent future: A promise of peace for ourselves, our families, and our world*. Novato, CA: New World Library.

National Association for Multicultural Education. (2001). *Criteria for evaluating state curriculum standards*. Retrieved from http://www.nameorg.org/resolutions/statecurr.html

National Association of Student Councils. (2015). *Raising student voice and participation*. Retrieved from http://www.nasc.us/raising-student-voice-participation/overview.aspx

National Center for Conflict Resolution Education. (2002). *The art in peacemaking: A guide to integrating conflict resolution education into youth arts programs*. Springfield, IL: Author.

National Council for the Social Studies. (2008). *A vision of powerful teaching and learning in the social studies: Building social understanding and civic efficacy* [Position statement]. Retrieved from http://www.socialstudies.org/positions/powerful

National Council for the Social Studies. (2012). *National curriculum standards for the social studies: Chapter 2—the themes of social studies*. Retrieved from http://www.socialstudies.org/standards/strands

National Women's History Project. (2007). *Pathbreakers*. Retrieved from http://www.nwhp.org/resourcecenter/pathbreakers.php

National Women's History Project. (2013). *Women inspiring innovation through imagination*. Retrieved from http://www.nwhp.org/

Naylor, N. (2008). Memorandum to directors of education, secretary/treasurers of school authorities. August 18. Ministry of Education,

Ontario, Canada. Retrieved from http://www.edu.gov.on.ca/eng/policyfunding/memos/august2008/B_10PeaceProgress.pdf

Ndura-Quédraogo, E., & Amster, R. (eds). (2009). *Building cultures of peace: Transdisciplinary voices of hope and action*. Newcastle-upon-Tyne, UK: Cambridge Scholars.

Nelson, T., & Coleman, C. (2011). Human-environmental relationships as curriculum context: An interdisciplinary inquiry. In J. Lin, & R. L. Oxford (Series eds), *Transforming Education for the Future Series: Vol. Transformative eco-education for human and planetary survival* (pp. 153–167). Charlotte, NC: Information Age.

The New Conversations Initiative. (2015). *Open source library*. Retrieved from http://www.newconversations.net

New York State Education Department. (2011). *Educating the whole child, engaging the whole (SEDL) in New York State*. Retrieved from http://www.p12.nysed.gov/sss/sedl/SEDLguidelines.pdf

Nicolescu, B. (2002). *Manifesto of transdisciplinarity* (K-C. Voss, trans.). Albany, NY: State University of New York.

Nieto, S. (2004). *Affirming diversity: The sociopolitical context of multicultural education* (4th edition). New York: Allyn & Bacon.

Noddings, N. (2008). Caring and peace education. In M. Bajaj (ed.), *Encyclopedia of peace education*. Charlotte, NC: Information Age. Retrieved from http://www.tc.edu/centers/epe/entries.html

Noddings, N. (2010). Moral education in an age of globalization. *Educational Philosophy and Theory*, 42(4), 390–396. doi:10.1111/j.1469-5812.2008.00487.x

Oakes, J., & Lipton, M. (1999). *Teaching to change the world*. New York, NY: McGraw-Hill.

Ochoa-Becker, A. S. (2007). *Democratic education for social studies: An issues-centered decision making curriculum*. Greenwich, CT: Information Age.

Odora Hoppers, C. A. (2002). Indigenous knowledge and the integration of knowledge systems: Towards a conceptual and methodological framework. In C. A. Odora Hoppers (ed.), *Indigenous knowledge and the integration of knowledge systems: Towards a philosophy of articulation* (pp. 2–22). Claremont, SA: New Africa Books.

Oetzel, J. G., & Ting-Toomey, S. (eds). (2013). *The SAGE Handbook of conflict communication: Integrating theory, research, and practice* (2nd edition). Thousand Oaks, CA: SAGE.

Office of the High Commissioner for Human Rights. (2004). *ABC: Teaching human rights. Practical activities for primary and secondary schools* (2nd edition). New York, United Nations. Available from http://www.un.org/wcm/webdav/site/visitors/shared/documents/pdfs/Pub_United%20Nations_ABC_human%20rights.pdf

Ohio Commission on Dispute Resolution and Conflict Management. (2009). *Conflict resolution education around the world, Germany*. Retrieved from http://worldcat.org/arcviewer/5/OHI/2011/07/07/H1310061821187/viewer/file614.htm

Ohio Commission on Dispute Resolution and Conflict Management. (2009). *Conflict resolution education around the world, Thailand*. Retrieved from http://worldcat.org/arcviewer/5/OHI/2011/07/07/H1310061821187/viewer/file751.htm

Orlick, (2008). *In pursuit of excellence: How to win in sport and life through mental training* (4th edition). Champaign, IL: Human Kinetics.

Oxford, R. (2013). *The language of peace: Communicating to create harmony*. Charlotte, NC: Information Publishing.

Oxford, R. L. (2011). Eco-fashion: What educators can and should teach about sustainable fashion. In J. Lin, & R. L. Oxford (eds), *Transformative eco-education for human and planetary survival* (pp. 309–334). Charlotte, NC: Information Age.

Pang, V. O., Fernekes, W. R., & Nelson, J. L. (eds). (2010). *The human impact of natural disasters: Issues for the inquiry-based classroom*. National Council for the Social Studies, Bulletin 110. Silver Spring, MD: National Council for the Social Studies.

Parker, W. C. (2003). The deliberative approach to education for democracy: Problems and possibilities. In J. J. Patrick, G. E. Hamot, & R. S. Leming (eds), *Civic learning in teacher education: International perspectives on education for democracy in the preparation of teachers*. Vol. 2. (pp. 99–115). Bloomington, IN: Educational Resources Information Center.

Pate, G. S. (1997). Research on reducing prejudice. In M. E. Haas, & M. A. Laughlin (eds), *Meeting the standards: Social studies readings for K-6 educators* (pp. 90–93). Washington, DC: National Council for the Social Studies.

Patrick, J. (1986). *Critical thinking in the social studies* (ERIC Digest No. 30). Retrieved from ERIC database: http://20.132.48.254/PDFS/ED272432.pdf

The Peace Alliance. (2013). *About the US Department of Peacebuilding*. June, 1. Retrieved from http://www.thepeacealliance.org/issues-advocacy/department-of-peace/

Pellegrino, A. M., & Lee, C. D. (2012). *Let the music play: Harnessing the power of music for history and social studies classrooms*. Charlotte, NC: Information Age.

Percoco, J. A. (2001). *Divided we stand: Teaching about conflict in U. S. history*. Portsmouth, NH: Heinemann.

Peters, M. A., & Britton, A. (2008). *Global citizenship education: Philosophy, theory and pedagogy*. Rotterdam: Sense.

Pirtle, S. (1998). *Linking up: Using music, movement, and language arts to promote caring, cooperation, and communication*. Cambridge, MA: Educators for Social Responsibility.

Polon, L., & Cantwell, A. (1983). *The whole earth holiday book*. Glenview, IL: Good Year Books.

Pranis, K. (2005). *The little book of circle processes: A new/old approach to peacemaking*. Intercourse, PA: Good Books.

Purkey, W. W. (2000). *What students say to themselves: Internal dialogue and school success*. Thousand Oaks, CA: Corwin.

Ramose, M. B. (1996). Specific African thought structures and their possible contribution to world peace. In H. Beck, & G. Schmirber (eds), *Creative peace through encounter of world cultures* (pp. 211–235). New Delhi, India: Sri Satguru Publications.

Read, H. (1949). *Education for peace*. New York, NY: Charles Scribner..

Reardon, B. A. (1988). *Comprehensive peace education: Educating for global responsibility*. New York, NY: Teachers College Press.

Reardon, B. A. (1995). *Educating for human dignity: Learning about rights and responsibilities*. Philadelphia, PA: University of Pennsylvania.

Reardon, B. A. (2001). *Education for a culture of peace in a gender perspective*. Paris, France: United Nations Educational, Scientific and Cultural Organization (UNESCO).

Reeves, D. B. (2002). *The leader's guide to standards: A blueprint for educational equity and excellence*. San Francisco, CA: Jossey-Bass.

Reynolds, D. B. (2002). *Taking the high road: Communities organize for economic change*. London: M. E. Sharpe.

Richards, J. C. (with Kroeger, D.). (2012). Transdisciplinarity: Shaping the future by reading the word and reading the world in an eighth grade classroom. *Reading Improvement*, 49(1), 6–16.

Rimington, J. (2013). The challenge. *One World Youth Project*. Retrieved from http://oneworldyouthproject.org/about-the-organization/vision/

Rosenberg, M. B. (2000). *Nonviolent communication: A language of compassion*. Encinitas, CA: PuddleDancer Press.

Rosenberg, M. B. (2003). *Life-enriching education: Nonviolent communication helps schools improve performance, reduce conflict, and enhance relationships*. Encinitas, CA: PuddleDancer.

Rosenberg, M. (2005). *Teaching children compassionately: How students and teachers can succeed with mutual understanding*. Encinitas, CA: PuddleDancer Press.

Rugg, H. O. (1931). *Culture and education in America*. New York: Harcourt Brace.

Rugg, H. O. (1939). Curriculum-design in the social studies: What I believe. In J. A. Michener (ed.), *The future of the social studies: Proposals for an experimental social-studies curriculum* (pp. 140–158). National Council for the Social Studies.

Saafir, M. (2012). Rhythm, rhyme, reel, resistance: Transformative learning using African American popular culture. In S. Kippers, & C. J. B. McGill (eds), *Pathways to transformation: Learning in relationship* (pp. 261–274). Charlotte, NC: Information Age.

Salazar, M. L. (1995). Peace education in the Denver public schools. A study of social studies classes in grade 7. *Peace Education Miniprints No. 78*. Malmo, Sweden: School of Education.

Sandlin, J. A., Kahn, R., Darts, D., & Tavin, K. (2009). To find the cost of freedom. Theorizing and practicing a critical pedagogy of consumption. *Journal of Critical Education Policy Studies*, 7(2), 98–125.

Sapon-Shevin, M. (2010). *Because we can change the world: A practical guide to building cooperative, inclusive classroom communities*. Thousand Oaks, CA: Corwin.

Sawatsky, J. (2008). *Just peace ethics: A guide to restorative justice and peacebuilding*. Eugene, OR: Cascade.

Scharf, A., & Bhagat, R. (2007). Arts and peace education: The Richmond Youth Peace Project. *Harvard Educational Review*, 77(3), 379–382.

Schocker, J. B., Croft, S., Licwinko, J., Muthersbaugh, P., Rossetti, G., & Yeager, M. (2012). Student teachers tackle the lack of social studies in urban elementary schools. *Ohio Social Studies Review*, 48(1), 20–32.

Seif, E. (2009). School for peace and justice. *Educational Leadership*, 66(10). Retrieved from http://www.ascd.org/publications/educational-leadership/jul09/vol66/num10/A-School-for-Peace-and-Justice.aspx

Shaban, M. (2012). *Peace education in Palestine*. Palestinian Development Curriculum Center. Retrieved from http://www.sauvescholars.org/uploads/Shaban,%20Peace%20Education%20in%20Palestine%20-%20Recommendations%20DRAFT.pdf

Shank, M. S., & Schirch, L. (2008). Strategic arts-based peacebuilding. *Peace & Change*, 33(2), 217–242. doi:10.1111/j.1468-0130.2008.00490.x

Sharp, G. (2012). Gender in the hidden curriculum (update). *Sociological Images*. Retrieved from http://thesocietypages.org/socimages/2012/11/16/gender-in-the-hidden-curriculum/

Sharra, S. (2006). Breaking the elephant's tusk: Teacher autobiography and methodology in peace education. *Journal of Stellar Peacemaking*, 1(3). Retrieved from http://74.127.11.121/peacejournal/volume_index/3/v1n3a7.html

Shor, J. (2004). *Born to buy: The commercialized child and the new consumer culture*. New York: Scribner.

Shor, I. (2007). What is critical literacy? *Journal for Pedagogy, Pluralism & Practice*, 1–25.

Silva, J. M., & Langhout, R. D. (2011). Cultivating agents of change in children. *Theory and Research in Social Education*, 39(1), 61–91.

Smit, B. (2003). *The emotional state of teachers during educational policy change*. Paper presented at the European Conference on Educational Research. University of Hamburg, Germany. September. Retrieved from http://www.leeds.ac.uk/educol/documents/00003200.htm

Smith A., & Robinson, A. (1996). *Education for mutual understanding: The initial statutory years*. Coleraine, Northern Ireland: Centre for the Study of Conflict, University of Ulster. Retrieved from http://cain.ulst.ac.uk/csc/reports/mutual.htm

Soka Gakkai International. (2014). *Charter of the Soka Gakkai International*. Retrieved from http://www.sgi.org/resource-center/introductory-materials/sgi-charter.html

Sommerfelt, O. H., & Vambheim, V. (2008). The dream of the good – a peace education project exploring the potential to educate for peace at an individual level. *Journal of Peace Education*, 5(1), 79–95.

Somerville, M. A., & Rapport, D. J. (eds). (2000). *Transdisciplinarity: Re-creating integrated knowledge*. Oxford, UK: Encyclopedia of Life Support Systems, Developed under the Auspices of the UNESCO Publishers.

Song, K. Y., & Muschert, G. W. (2014). Opening the contemplative mind in the sociology classroom. *Humanity & Society*, 38(3), 314–338.

Souto-Manning, M. (2009). Negotiating culturally responsive pedagogy through multicultural children's literature: Towards critical democratic literacy practices in a first grade classroom. *Journal of Early Childhood Literacy*, 9(1), 74–93. doi:10.1177/1468798408101105

Spurgeon, C. (1998). Citizenship education through literature. In C. Holden and N. Clough (eds), *Children as citizens: Education for participation* (pp. 127–137). Philadelphia: Kingsley.

Starhawk. (1987). *Truth or dare: Encounters with power, authority and mystery*. San Francisco: Harper & Row.

Stevahn, S., Johnson, D. W., Johnson, R. T., & Schultz, R. (2002). Effects of conflict resolution training integrated into a high school social studies curriculum. *The Journal of Social Psychology*, 142(3), 305–331.

Stone, L. (2000). Embodied identity: Citizenship education for American girls. In M. Arnot, & J. Dillabough (eds), *Challenging democracy: International perspectives on gender, education and citizenship* (pp. 73–86). New York: Routledge.

Szpara, M. Y., & Ahmad, I. (2006). *Making social studies meaningful for ELL students: Content and pedagogy in mainstream secondary school classrooms*. Retrieved from http://www.usca.edu/essays/vol162006/ahmad.pdf

Teaching Tolerance. (2013). *Classroom resources*. Teaching Tolerance: A Project of the Southern Poverty Law Center. Retrieved from http://www.tolerance.org/classroom-resources

Thoreau, H. D. (1848). *On the duty of civil disobedience*. Lecture at the Concord Lyceum. Retrieved from http://www.panarchy.org/thoreau/disobedience.1848.html

Thornton, S. (2007). *Futurism cardboard sculpture*. Retrieved from http://sabrinasbest.tripod.com/id28.html

Thornton, S. J. (2004). Citizenship education and social studies curriculum change after 9/11. In S. J. Thornton (ed.), *Social education in the twentieth century: Curriculum and context for citizenship* (pp. 210–220). New York, NY: Peter Lang.

Thornton, S. J. (2005). *Teaching social studies that matter: Curriculum for active learning*. New York, NY: Teachers College.

Thrupp, M., & Tomlinson, S. (2005). Introduction: Educational policy, social justice and "complex hope." *British Educational Research Journal*, 31(5), 549–556.

Toffler, A. (ed.). (1974). *Learning for tomorrow: The role of the future in education*. New York, NY: Random House.

Tomovska, A. (2009). Social context and contact hypothesis: Perceptions and experiences of a contact program for ten-to eleven-year-old children in the Republic of Macedonia. In C. McGlynn, M. Zemblas, Z. Bekerman, & A. Gallgher (eds), *Peace education and post-conflict societies: Comparative perspectives* (pp. 138–160). New York: Palgrave Macmillan.

Tonkinson, R. (2004). Resolving conflict within the law: The Mardu Aborigines of Australia. In G. Kemp, & D. P. Fry (eds), *Keeping the peace: Conflict resolution and peaceful societies around the world* (pp. 73–86). New York, NY: Routledge.

Totten, S. (1997). Teaching the Holocaust story to children. In M. E. Haas, & M. A. Laughlin (eds), *Meeting the standards: Social studies readings for K-6 educators* (pp. 61–63). Washington, DC: National Council for the Social Studies.

Totten, S. (2012). A synergy of awareness, understanding, empathy and action: Confronting social issues in the English classroom and beyond. In S. Totten, & J. E. Pedersen (eds), *Researching and teaching social issues: The personal stories and pedagogical efforts of professors of education* (pp. 207–236). Charlotte, NC: Information Age.

Totten, S., & Pedersen, J. E. (eds). (2011). *Educating about social issues in the 20th and 21st Centuries. A critical annotated bibliography.* Vol. 1. Charlotte, NC: Information Age.

Totten, S., & Pedersen, J. E. (eds). (2012). *Researching and teaching social issues: The personal stories and pedagogical efforts of professors of education.* Charlotte, NC: Information Age.

Totten, S., & Pedersen, J. E. (2013). *Educating about social issues in the 20th and 21st centuries: A critical annotated bibliography* (Vol. 2). Charlotte, NC: Information Age.

Twine, F. (1994). *Citizenship and social rights: The interdependence of self and society.* London: Sage.

United Nations. (1989). *Convention on the rights of the child.* Office of the High Commissioner for Human Rights. Retrieved from http://www.ohchr.org/Documents/ProfessionalInterest/crc.pdf

United Nations Educational, Scientific and Cultural Organization. (1998). *International decade for a culture of peace and non-violence for the children of the world, 2001–2010.* Resolution 53/25. November, 19. Retrieved from http://www3.unesco.org/iycp/uk/uk_sum_decade.htm

United Nations Educational, Scientific and Cultural Organization. (2012). *Building peace in the minds of men and women.* Retrieved from http://www.unesco.org/new/en/unesco/

United Nations General Assembly. (1998). *Culture of peace* (A/RES/52/13). January, 15. Retrieved from http://www3.unesco.org/iycp/uk/uk_sum_decade.htm

Utset, M., Villanueva, M., & Gonzalo, C. (1998). Consumers as citizens: Children working together across Europe. In C. Holden, & N. Clough (eds), *Children as citizens: Education for participation* (pp. 228–239). Philadelphia, PA: Kingsley.

Verhagen, F. C. (2004). Contextual sustainability education: Towards an integrated educational framework for social and ecological peace. In A. L. Wenden (ed.), *Educating for a culture of social and ecological peace* (pp. 53–76). Albany, NY: State University of New York Press.

Vinson, K. D., Ross, E. W., & Wilson, M. B. (2012). Standards-based educational reform and social studies education: A critical introduction. In W. B. Russell III (ed.), *Contemporary social studies: An essential reader* (pp. 153–172). Charlotte, NC: Information Age.

Vogler, K. (2003). Where does social studies fit in a high-stakes testing environment. *Social Studies*, 94(5), 207–211. doi:10.1080/00377990309600208

Wade, R. C. (2007). *Social studies for social justice: Teaching strategies for the elementary classroom*. New York, NY: Teachers College Press.

Wakhlu, A. (1999). *Managing from the heart: Unfolding spirit in people and organizations*. Thousand Oaks, CA: Response.

Walsh, D. (1997). Critical thinking to reduce prejudice. In M. E. Haas, & M. A. Laughlin (eds), *Meeting the standards: Social studies readings for k-6 educators* (pp. 98–101). Washington, DC: National Council for the Social Studies.

Wangoola, P. (2006). The indigenous child: The Afrikan philosophical and spiritual basis of honoring children. In R. Cavoukian, & S. Olfman (eds), *Child honoring: How to turn this world around* (pp. 117–126). London: Praeger.

Wannawichitra, C., Ruenwongsa, P., Ketpichainarong, W., & Jittam, P. (2011). Development of an integrated learning unit for enhancing awareness and conceptual understanding of global warming in secondary students. *The International Journal of Learning*, 17(11), 399–415.

Washington, E. Y., & Humphries, E. K. (2011). A social studies teacher's sense making of controversial issues discussions of race in a predominantly white, rural high school classroom. *Theory and Research in Social Education*, 39(1), 92–114.

Waterson, R. A., & Haas, M. E. (2011). Dare we not teach 9/11 yet advocate citizenship education. *Social Studies*, 102(4), 147. doi:10.1080/00377996.2011.584281

Weatherford, J. (1997) Indian season in American schools. In M. E. Haas, & M. A. Laughlin (eds), *Meeting the standards: Social studies readings for educators* (pp. 32–36). Washington, DC: National Council for the Social Studies.

Weaver, J. D., & Biesecker-Mast, G. (eds). (2003). *Teaching peace: Nonviolence and the liberal arts*. Lanham, MD: Rowman and Littlefield.

Weems, M. E. (2003). *Public education and the imagination-intellect: I speak from the wound in my mouth*. New York: Peter Lang.

Weil, D. K. (1998). *Towards a critical multicultural literacy: Theory and practice for education for liberation*. New York, NY: Peter Lang.

Welch, C. A. (2001). *Children of the Civil Rights Era*. Minneapolis: Carolrhoda.

Wenden, A. L. (ed.). (2004). *Educating for a culture of social and ecological peace*. Albany, NY: State University of New York Press.

West Africa Network for Peacebuilding. (2013). Experts meeting to develop policy framework on peace education in plateau state. *News & Events*. Retrieved from http://www.wanep.org/wanep/news-a-events-wanep-updates/395.html

Westwood, P. (2011). *Commonsense methods for children with special educational needs* (6th edition). New York: Routledge.

Wickett, R. E. Y. (2005). The spiritual and human learning. In P. Jarvis, & S. Parker (eds), *Human learning: An holistic approach* (pp. 157–167). New York, NY: Routledge.

Williams, L. K. (1995). It's okay to feel. *Can-Do! Kids: Conflict Management* (Music & lyrics) Retrieved from http://www.songsforteaching.com/store/can-do-kids-conflict-management-mini-album-download-pr-58273.html

Williams, L. K. (1996). *Caring and capable kids* (Cassette). Retrieved from http://peacemaker.st/LKW/index.html

Williams, L. K. (1996). *Caring and capable kids*. Retrieved from http://peacemaker.st/LKW/index.html (This is a companion book of the recording by the same title. Book includes music and corresponding activities.)

Wilson, W., & Papadonis, J. (2006). *Differentiated instruction for social studies: Instructions and activities for the diverse classroom*. Portland, ME: Walch.

Women's International League for Peace and Freedom. (2013). Outer space. Retrieved from http://www.reachingcriticalwill.org/resources/fact-sheets/critical-issues/5448-outer-space

World Movement for Democracy (2014). Teaching civic education in and outside of school. Author. Retrieved from http://www.wmd.org/resources/whats-being-done/civic-education-democracy/teaching-civic-education-and-outside-school

World Social Forum. (2002). *Charter of principles*. Retrieved from http://www.forumsocialmundial.org.br/main.php?id_menu=4&cd_language=2

Yablon, Y. B. (2006). The role of emotions in peace-building activities. In Y. Iram, H. Wahrman, & Z. Gross (eds), *Educating toward a culture of peace* (pp. 207–222). Charlotte, NC: Information Age.

Yeh, T. D. (2006). The way to peace: A Buddhist perspective. *International Journal of Peace Studies*, 11(1), 91–112. Retrieved from http://www.gmu.edu/programs/icar/ijps/vol11_1/11n1Yeh.pdf

Yogev, E. (2010). History curriculum with multiple narratives. In C. C. Carter, & R. Kumar (eds), *Peace philosophy in action* (pp. 79–103). New York, NY: Palgrave Macmillan.

Zembylas, M., & Bekerman, Z. (2013). Peace education in the present: Dismantling and reconstructing some fundamental theoretical premises. *Journal of Peace Education*, 10(2), 197–214. doi: 10.1080/17400201.2013.790253

Zembylas, M., & McGlynn, C. (2012). Discomforting pedagogies: Emotional tensions, ethical dilemmas and transformative possibilities. *British Educational Research Journal*. 38(1), 41–59. doi:10.1080/01411926.2010.523779/

Name Index

A Guide for Training Study Circle Facilitators, 69
Abernot, Yvan, 57, 146
Adams, Caralee, 114, 130
Adams, David, 15, 130
Adler, Susan, 26, 116, 130
Adwan, Sami, 78, 132
Ahmad, Iftikhar, 80, 157
Alaska Native Knowledge Network, 130
Alaska Standards for Culturally Responsive Schools, 45
Alleman, Janet, 74, 80, 83, 130, 133
Allen, Barb, 58, 138
American Educational Research Association, 16, 135
Amnesty International, 96, 116, 131
Amster, Randall, 48, 151
Amstutz, Lorraine, 9, 131
Anderson, Derek L., 105, 131
Andrzejewski, Julie, 93, 131
Anti-Defamation League, 39
Apple, Michael, 98, 131
Arnold, Harriett, 22, 82, 139
Arsenio, William F., 83, 147
Artists Culture of Peace, 26, 69
Ashoka's Youth Venture, 100, 118
Assembly of Alaska Native Educators, 131

Atkin, Beth S., 80, 89
Au, Wayne, 51, 101, 131
Aung San Suu Kyi, 11
Avery, Patricia G., 110, 131

Bae, Jaehan, 131
Baltodano, Marta P., 131
Banks, James A., 50, 75, 96, 131, 132, 140
Bar-On, Dan, 78, 132
Bartkowski, Marcie J., 69, 113, 132
Basile, Carole, 105, 132
Bekerman, Zvi, 3, 4, 157, 161
Bellah, Robert N., 6, 108, 132
Bendik-Keymer, Jeremy, 107, 108, 132
Berdan, Kristina, 53, 132
Berry, Thomas, 21, 132, 145
Bertling, Joy, 64, 132
Bhagat, Ram, 19, 155
Bible Study Tools, 7, 132
Biesecker-Mast, Gerald, 85, 160
Bigelow, William "Bill", 63, 96, 101, 112, 131, 132
Boulding, Elise, 12, 17, 69, 81, 102, 132, 133
Boulding, Kenneth, 102, 133
Boulton, Ian, 132
Bourdieu, Pierre, 57, 133
Bowers, Chet, 107, 133
Boyle-Baise, Marilynne, 84, 133
Brameld, Theodore, 13, 133

Branscomb, Kathryn R., 83, 139
Brantmeier, Edward J., 7, 114, 133, 140, 149
Braungart, Margaret M., 79, 133
Braungart, Richard G., 79, 133
Britton, Alan, 109, 153
Brophy, Jere, 53, 74, 80, 83, 130, 133
Brown, David F., 80, 89, 133
Bstan-'Dzin-Rgy (See Dalai Lama), 98, 102, 118, 133, 137
Buddhism, 10, 14, 15
Buddist, 10, 11, 15, 161
Burke, Amy L., 94, 133
Butroyd, Bob, 31, 133
Butzow, Carol M., 106, 134
Butzow, John W., 106, 134

Cairns, Ed, 148
California Department of Education, 38, 49, 134
Callendar, Christine, 115, 134
Camicia, Steven P., 48, 62, 134
Campbell, Sarah, 59, 134
Canfield, Jack, 23, 26, 85, 89, 116, 134, 135
Cannon, Susan Gelber, 48, 64, 114, 134
Cantwell, Aileen, 59, 154
Cardoso, Onelio Jorge, 95, 134
Carter, Candice C., 1, 2, 6, 9, 22, 26, 29, 37, 47, 58, 60, 72, 73, 74, 85, 89, 92, 94, 99, 113, 115, 129, 134, 135, 161
Catterall, James S., 102, 135
Cavanagh, Tom, 9, 135
Cavoukian, Raffi, 146, 149, 159
Center for Contemplative Mind in Society, 61, 135
Center for Nonviolent Communication, 55, 135
Chandler, Prentice, 63, 135, 136
Charalambous, Constadina, 30, 136
Charalambous, Panayiota, 30, 136
Charter of the Soka Gakkai International, 14
Chittenden Central Supervisory Union, 136
Christensen, Linda, 13, 136

Chugoku Shimbun, 145
Clark, Don, 65, 136
Cleary, Linda Miller, 104, 136
Coleman, Cynthia, 77, 151
Collaborative for Academic, Social, and Emotional Learning, 39, 89, 118, 136
Comer, James P., 81, 136
Constitutional Rights Foundation, 13, 136
Cornbleth, Catherine, 81, 136
Cortés, Carlos E., 17, 98, 136
Counts, George S., 13, 136
Cranton, Patricia, 61, 136
Crawford, Patricia, 60, 137
Crocco, Margaret, 48, 96, 131, 136, 137
Croft, Stephen, 155
Cruz, Barbara, 80, 137
Culture of Peace Resolution, 35
Curti, Merle Eugene, 6, 137

D'Ambrosio, Ubiratan, 77, 137
Dajani, Mohammed, 6, 137
Dalai Lama, 98, 102, 118, 133, 137
Daly, Herman E., 107, 137
Danesh, Hosain B., 14, 78, 137
Darder, Antonia, 59, 137
Darling, Farr L., 101, 137
Darts, David, 155
de los Reyes, Eileen, 17, 137
DePaul, Savarimuthu Vincent, 30, 138
De Pauw, Linda Grant, 52, 69, 138
Decade for Peace, 35
Dewey, John, 13, 50, 138, 139
Diamond, Louise, 6, 65, 112, 132, 138
Diem, Richard, 48, 138
Diller, Jerry V., 104, 138
Donnison, David, 108, 138
Doppen, Frans, 48, 150
Dresser, Norine, 105, 138
Dr. Martin Luther King Jr., 60
Dryzek, John S., 102, 108, 138
the Dream, 9
Duckworth, Cheryl Lynn, 58, 138
Dukkha Niroda Gamini Patipada, 11
Dumais, Susan A., 57, 138

Name Index

Earth Charter, 21, 26, 35, 36, 118, 138
Earth and Peace Education Associates, 138
Earth Charter Initiative, 2, 35, 138
Eastern Philosophies, 5, 10
Easterners, 11
Educating Beyond Violent Futures, 144
Education for Mutual Understanding, 37
Education for Peace International, 138
Educators for Social Responsibility, 89, 142, 154
Egan, Kieran, 77, 138
Eidman-Aadahl, Elyse, 132
Eisler, Riane, 63, 81, 139, 143, 145
Eisner, Elliot W., 18, 139
Eldridge, Michael, 51, 139
Elias, Maurice J., 22, 82, 139
Emerson, Kirk, 106, 139
Enslin, Penny, 78, 148
Envisioning the Peaceable Kingdom, 17, 133
Epstein, Terrie, 63, 139
Ethridge, Elizabeth A., 83, 139
Etzioni, Amitai, 81, 139
Evans, Ronald W., 62, 139

Farley, Joshua, 107, 137
Federation of Bosnia and Herzegovina, 37
Fernekes, William R., 52, 153
Finley, Laura L., 77, 139
Fisk, Larry, 19, 139
Fitchett, Paul G., 33, 139
Fleming, Jennie, 132
Florida Department of Education, 38, 140
Fogarty, Robin J., 74, 140
Foster, John Bellamy, 77, 140
Four Arrows (Jacobs, Don Trent), 14, 140
Four Arrows & Mann, Barbara Alice, 14, 140
Four Noble Truths, 11
Freire, Paulo, 13, 101, 140
Friedrich, Patricia, 56, 140

Fritzsche, K. Peter, 84, 140
Fromm, Erich, 111, 140

Galinsky, Ellen, 17, 140
Gallagher, Anthony, 37
Galtung, Johan, 12, 50, 82, 102, 140
Gandhi, 10–12, 20, 106
Gardner, Howard, 84, 140
Gardner, Launie, 132
Gaudelli, William, 131
Gautama, 10
Gay, Geneva, 62, 140
Germany, 39, 152, 156
Gernstein, Lawrence H., 62, 140
Ghaderi, Mostafa, 63, 141
Giddens, Anthony, 112, 141
Gilbert, Jenelle N., 56, 141
Giroux, Henry A., 13, 141
Glass, Kathy, 62, 141
Global Exchange, 110, 141
Global Network Against Weapons and Nuclear Power in Space, 141
Goel, Lakshmi, 54, 141
Goldberg, Tsafrir, 78, 141
Golston, Syd, 50, 141
Gomes de Matos, Francisco, 56, 141
Gonzalo, Carmen, 113, 159
Goodall, Jane, 103, 118, 142
Gottlieb, Robert, 106, 142
Gozemba, Patricia, 17, 137
Graczyk, Patricia A., 139
Great Peace, 8, 26
Greene, Maxine, 17, 142
Grice, James, 77, 142
Grolnick, Maureen, 131
Gross, Fred E., 77, 89
Gross, Zehavit, 36, 132, 137, 140, 142, 145, 161
Guidelines for Teaching About American Indian History, 53

Haas, Mary, 52, 131, 153, 158–160
Haavelsrud, Magnus, 78, 142
Hadley, Michael L., 9, 142
Hague Appeal for Peace, 35, 36
Hahn, Carole, 82, 142

Halpern, Charles, 116, 142
Hansen, Mark Victor, 26, 89, 134, 135
Harris, Ian M., 6, 12, 18, 19, 22, 61, 135, 142, 143, 149
Harrison, Jane, 98, 147
Harste, Jerome C., 64, 143
Hart, Sura, 55, 97, 143
Hart, Tobin, 61, 143
Hawkins, Kevin, 94, 133
Heafner, Tina L., 33, 96, 139, 143
Heath, Douglas H., 77, 143
Helmsing, Mark, 65, 143
Henderson, Hazel, 113, 143
Herborn, Peter J., 85, 144
Herd, Denise A., 113, 143
Herndon, Akbar Ali, 61, 143
Hester, Casey, 65, 143
Hewstone, Miles, 148
Hicks, David, 102, 143
Hill, Clifford, 61, 143
Hiroshima, 38, 111, 145
Hodson, Victoria Kindle, 97, 143
Hoffman, Gene Knudsen, 55, 143
Holmwood, John, 143
hooks, bell, 55, 144
Hopkins, Belinda, 59, 144
Howarth, Thomas Edward Brodie, 115, 144
Hyland, Terry, 95, 144
Human Rights Education Association, 39
Humphries, Emma, 81, 159
Hursh, David W., 96, 144
Hutchinson, Francis P., 14, 85, 144

Ikeda, Daisaku, 103, 144
Immanuel Kant, 12, 145, 146
Indigenous Peoples of North America, 8
Industrial Workers of the World, 63
International Cities of Peace, 19, 144
the International Decade for a culture of Peace and Non-Violence for the Children of the World, 15, 158

International Network for Education in Emergencies, 144
International Peace Research Association, 144
Iram, Yaacov, 36, 132, 137, 140, 145, 161
Iroquois Confederacy, 8
Ives, Blake, 141

Jainism, 10
Japan, 38, 111, 144
Japanese Teens in Hiroshima, 111, 145
Jittam, Piyachat, 159
John Amos Comenius, 11
Johnson, David W., 145, 157
Johnson, Norman, 141
Johnson, Roger T., 145, 157
Jones, Van, 106, 145
Journal of Peace Education, 4, 16, 134–138, 142, 143, 148, 156, 161
Junglas, Iris, 141

Kahn, Richard, 111
Kahne, Joseph E., 116, 145
Kant, Immanuel, 12, 145, 146
Karp, Stan, 101, 131
Karpinska, Zuki, 61, 143
Keating, Joshua, 40, 145
Keen, Sam, 53, 69, 145
Kendall, Clare, 109, 145
Kerr, David, 113, 145
Kessler, Rachel, 66, 145
Ketpichainarong, Watcharee, 159
Kids for Peace, 16, 145
Kids for Peace Pledge, 16
Kimura, Takeshi, 21, 145
Kincheloe, Joe, 32, 33, 104, 146
King, Martin Luther, 11, 60, 108
Kleingeld, Pauline, 12, 146
Knighton, Barbara, 80, 130
Konidari, Victoria, 57, 146
Korn-Bursztyn, Carol, 146
Korten, David, 112, 146
Korty, Carol, 56, 146
Kramer, William R., 74, 146
Kreisberg, Seth, 101, 146
Krieger, David, 142, 144, 146

Name Index

Kumar, Ravindra, 6, 135, 161
Kumashiro, Kevin, 114, 146

Lakota People, 8
Langhout, Regina Day, 34, 156
Lappin, Richard, 73, 146
Larson, Colleen L., 104, 146
Lederach, John P., 7, 147
Lee, Najuana P., 58, 84, 89, 147, 153
Lemerise, Elizabeth A., 83, 147
Levin, Tamar, 73, 147
Levinson Bradley A. U., 114, 147
Levinson, Meira, 115, 147
Lewis, Barbara A., 87, 147
Licwinko, Jennifer, 155
Lieber, Carol M., 60, 147
Lin, Jing, 7, 21, 55, 133, 140, 147, 149, 151, 153
Linklater, Andrew, 101, 147
Lintner, Timothy, 76, 147
Lipietz, Alain, 108
Lipton, Martin, 42, 152
Lonberger, Rosemary, 98, 147
Lovejoy, Nick, 55, 145
Lubig, Joe, 105, 131
Lynn, Erickson H., 64, 148

MacGinty, Roger, 9, 148
MacPhee, Deborah A., 64, 148
Madsen, Richard, 132
Maebuta, Jack, 77, 148
Maio, Mary, 23, 54, 148
Mandela, 11, 116
Mansfield Independent School District, 114
Marri, Anand Reddy, 110, 131
Marshall, Harriet, 51, 148
Martí, José, 94
Martin Luther King Jr., 11, 60, 108
Mason, DeWayne A., 74, 135
Mathis, Janelle B., 9, 148
Maxwell, Anne-Marie, 78, 148
Maxwell, Tudor, 78, 148
Mayors for Peace, 38
McGlynn, Claire, 65, 78, 148, 157, 161
McKnight, Douglas, 63, 135, 136

McLaren, Peter, 42, 148
Meidl, Christopher, 78, 148
Meidl, Tynisha, 78, 148
Mengual, Gloria Francesca, 59, 149
Merchant, Carolyn, 77, 149
Merideth, Robert, 106, 139
Merryfield, Merry, 48, 149
Middle Way, 10
Mikkelson, Patricia, 96, 149
Miller, John P., 133, 140, 149
Miller, Mary, 55, 149
Miller, Ron, 64, 143, 145, 149
Mindfulness Awareness Research Center, 118, 149
Ministerio de Educación Nacional Republic de Colombia, 36
Minteer, Ben A., 107, 109, 142, 149
Mirk, Paula, 60, 149
Mische, Patricia, 22, 149
Misco, Thomas, 48, 150
Moaz, Ifat, 99, 150
Moescheberger, Scott L., 62, 140
Mohism, 11
Montessori, 12, 62, 66, 78, 150
  Pedagogy of, 12
Morgan, Brian, 27, 62, 150
Morningside Center for Teaching Social Responsibility, 114, 150
Morrison, Mary Lee, 18, 19, 135, 143
Mobjörk, Malin, 73, 150
Morton, Patrick, 77, 89, 142
Moule, Jean, 104, 138
Movius, Hal, 106, 139
Mozi, 11
Mucklow, Nancy, 78, 150
Muller, Ray, 62, 150
Mullet, Judith Hostetler, 9, 131
Murphy, Gerald, 8, 150
Muschert, Glenn W., 94, 156
Mustafa, Javed, 78, 150
Muthersbaugh, Pamela, 155
Myanmar, 11
Myles, Brenda Smith, 57, 150

Nabhan, Gary Paul, 105, 151
Nabudere, Dani W., 73, 151

Name Index

Nagasaki, 38
Nagel, Greta, 10, 151
Nagler, Michael N., 6, 151
National Association for Multicultural Education, 151
National Association of Student Councils, 114
National Center for Conflict Resolution Education, 102, 151
National Commission for Basic Education, 38
National Council for the Social Studies, 2, 49, 50, 74, 80, 82, 83, 139, 151, 153, 155
National Public Telecomputing Network, 8, 150
National Women's History Project, 58, 69, 115, 118, 151
Naylor, Nancy, 37, 151
Ndura-Quédraogo, Elavie, 48, 151
Nelson, Jack L., 52, 77, 151, 153
Nevo, Yael, 73, 147, , 150
New York State Education Department, 31, 82
Nicolescu, Basarab, 73, 152
Niens, Ulrike, 148
Nieto, Sonia, 104, 152
Nirvana, 10
Nobel Peace Prize, 11
Noddings, Nel, 16, 66, 152
North American Association for Environmental Education, 39

Oakes, Jeannie, 42, 152
Ochoa-Becker, Anna S., 152
Odora Hoppers, Catherine A., 8, 152
Oetzel, John G., 81, 152
Office of the High Commissioner for Human Rights, 116
Ohio Commission on Dispute Resolution and Conflict Management, 37, 39, 152, 153
Olfman, Sharna, 146, 149, 159
One World Youth Project, 103, 154
Ong, Carah, 142, 144, 146

Ontario Ministry of Education in Canada, 37
Orey, Michael, 149
Orlick, Terry, 56
Ovando, Carlos J., 104, 146
Oxford, Rebecca L., 21, 22, 56, 147, 151, 153

Palomares, Susanna, 26, 89, 134, 135
Pang, Valerie Ooka, 52, 153
Papadonis, Jack, 62, 160
Parker, Walter C., 66, 153, 160
PassageWays curriculum, 66
Passeron, Jean Claude, 57, 133
Pate, Glenn S., 7, 153
Patrick, John J., 81, 153
Patterson, Nancy, 48, 150
Peace Education Commission, 16
Peace Education Special Interest Group, 16
Peace Education Standard, 32, 41, 42, 46, 126
Peace Seeds Newsletter, 111, 145
Peacock, Thomas D., 104, 136
Pedersen, Jon E., 62, 90, 93, 131, 142, 158
Pellegrino, Anthony M., 84, 153
Percoco, James A., 109, 153
Peters, Michael A., 109, 153
Pickett, Linda, 115, 135
Pirtle, Sarah, 98, 154
Poliner, Rachel A., 77, 89, 142
Polon, Linda, 59, 154
Pranis, Kay, 9, 60, 154
President Eisenhower, 23
Proverbs, 7
Perez, L. King, 80, 89
Purkey, William W., 21, 154

Radner, Hilary, 143
Ramose, Mogobe B., 8, 154
Rapport, David J., 73, 156
Read, Herbert, 19, 154
Reardon, Betty A., 13, 101, 110, 154
Reeves, Douglas B., 31, 154
Remy, Richard C., 48, 149
Resolution 53/25, 35, 118, 158

Rethinking Schools, 13
Reynolds, David B., 113, 154
Richmond Peace Education Center, 69
Richards, Janet C., 73, 154
Rimington, Jessica, 103, 154
Robinson, Stacey, 37, 105, 132, 156
Ron, Yiftach, 78, 141
Rogers, Iana, 132
Rosenberg, Marshall B., 34, 55, 96, 154, 155
Ross, Wayne E., 30, 96, 144, 159
Rossetti, Gabriela, 155
Ruenwongsa, Pintip, 159
Rugg, Harold O., 51, 63, 155

Saafir, Malik, 58, 265
Saavedra, Cinthya M., 48, 62, 134
Salazar, Mary Lou, 20, 155
Salmond, Kimberlee, 17, 140
Sandlin, Jennifer A., 111
Sanskrit, 10, 11
Sapon-Shevin, Mara, 42, 155
Sawatsky, Jarem, 108, 155
Saxe, David Warren, 62, 139
Schelvan, R. L., 57, 150
Scharf, Adria, 19, 155
Schirch, Lisa, 19, 110, 155
Schocker, Jessica, 48, 155
Schools of Hope, 76, 77, 143
Schulze, Gerhard, 143
Schultz, Ray, 157
Schweder, Windy, 76, 147
Seif, Elliott, 77, 155
Shaban, Mohammed, 155
Sandlin, Jennifer, A., 111
Shank, Michael, 19, 110, 155
Sharp, Gwen, 57, 155
Sharra, Steve, 8, 156
Shor, Ira, 52, 156
Shor, Juliet, 111, 156
Shuttleworth, Jay, 131
Silva, Janelle M., 34, 156
Simmons, Annette M., 110, 131
Smit, Brigitte, 30, 156

Smith, Alan, 37, 115, 156
Soka Gakkai (see also Value Creation Society), 15
Soka Gakkai International, 10, 14, 15, 144, 156
Solomon, Asali, 132, 148
Somerville, Margaret A., 73, 156
Sommerfelt, Ole Henning, 99, 156
Song, Kirsten Y., 94, 156
Souto-Manning, Mariana, 13, 156
Sporte, Susan E., 116, 145
Spurgeon, Chris, 98, 156
St. Augustine, 103
Standards for School Administrators, 128
Starhawk, 17, 157
Stenberg, Oddbjorn, 78, 142
Stevahn, Laurie, 113, 157
Stoehr, Judy, 74, 140
Stone, Lynda, 115, 157
Sulkunen, Pekka, 143
Sullivan, William M., 132
Swidler, Ann, 132
Symcox, Linda, 131
Szpara, Michelle Yvonne, 80, 157

Tao (the Way), 10, 28, 151
Taoism, 10, 151
Tavin, Kevin, 155
Taylor, Bob Pepperman, 107, 109, 142, 149, 157
Teacher Standard Number 8, 42
Teacher Standard Number 9, 43
Teachers Without Borders, 39, 118
Teaching Tolerance, 13, 119, 157
The Center for Nonviolent communication, 55, 135
The Dalai Lama Foundation, 102, 118, 137
The Establishment of Liberatory Alliances with People of Color, 59
The Hague Appeal for Peace, 35, 36
The National Women's History Project, 58
The New Conversations Initiative, 55, 157
The Peace Alliance, 116, 153

Name Index

The Rights of the Child, 36, 45, 116, 158
The Tirana Call for Peace Education, 36, 142
The Tree of Contemplative Practices, Thoreau, 157
Thomas, Nelson, 52, 77, 151
Thornton, Sabrina, 18
Thornton, Stephen J., 50, 80, 84
Thrupp, Martin, 31
Ting-Toomey, Stella, 81, 152
Tipton, Steven M., 132
Toffler, Alvin, 13
Tomlinson, Sally, 31, 157
Tomovska, Ana, 99, 157
Tonkinson, Robert, 9, 158
Totten, Samuel, 52, 62, 77, 90, 142, 158
Trautman, Retta C., 57, 150
Tree of Contemplative Practices, 61
Twine, France Winddance, 112, 158

Udayakumar, S. P., 50, 140
UNESCO, 35, 45, 118, 154, 156, 158
UNICEF, 45, 119
United Nations, 15, 35, 36, 44, 116, 119, 152, 154, 158
United Nations Convention of Children's Rights, 36, 44
United Nations Convention on The Rights of the Child, 36, 44
United Nations General Assembly, 35, 158
United States of America, 36, 38, 39, 61, 116
Urban Improv, 69
Utset, Marial Iglesias, 113, 159

Value Creation Society (see also Soka Gakkai), 15
Vambheim, Nils Vidar, 99, 156
Vandrick, Stephanie, 62, 150
Vavrus, Jessica, 45
Verhagen, Frans C., 40, 109, 159
Villanueva, M., 113, 159
Vinson, Kevin D., 30, 159
Vogler, Kenneth, 48, 159

Wade, Rahima C., 42, 83, 101, 159
Wahrman, Hillel, 36, 132, 137, 140, 145, 161
Wakhlu, Arun, 113, 159
Walsh, Debbie, 95, 159
Wangoola, Paulo, 109, 159
Wannawichitra, Chanintorn, 77, 159
Washington, Elizabeth Yeager, 81, 159
Waterson, Robert A., 52, 159
Weatherford, Jack, 27, 53, 160
Weaver, Denny J., 85, 160
Weems, Mary E., 17
Weil, Danny K., 104, 160
Weissberg, Roger P., 139
Welch, Catherine A., 115, 160
Wenden, Anita L., 21, 109, 159, 160
West Africa Network for Peacebuilding, 38, 160
Western Education, 61
Western Ideologies, 5, 11
Westerners, 10, 11, 13
Westwood, Peter, 62, 160
Wheeler, Gilda, 45
White, Cameron, 105, 132
Whitecotton, Emily J., 64, 148
Wickett, R. E. Y., 79, 160
Wicklund, Freeman, 93, 131
Williams, Linda, 26, 84, 89, 94, 95, 101, 134, 135, 160
Williams, Teri Triguba, 58, 138
Wilson, Melissa B., 27, 30, 62, 159
Winch, Bradley, 26, 89, 134, 135
Women's International League for Peace and Freedom, 6, 160
World Movement for Democracy, 160
World Social Forum, 15, 161
Wright, Cecile, 115, 134

Yablon, Yaacov B., 83, 161
Yeager, Melissa, 155
Yeh, Theresa Der-lan, 10, 161
Yogev, Esther, 14, 78, 161

Zembylas, Michalinos, 65, 161
Zevin, Jack, 84, 133

Subject Index

active learners, 83, 144, 157
active listening, 22, 42, 55, 101, 122
active social education, 83
aesthetic sign system, 64
Ahimsa, 10
affect, 109
affective education, 27
affective realm of learning, 65
agency, 27
arts, 18, 19, 24, 25, 28, 34, 40, 51, 58, 59, 64, 76, 80, 84, 86, 102, 134, 142, 146, 151, 154, 155, 160
arts expression, 102
attitude, 41, 65, 79, 97, 98, 99, 148
awareness, 4, 9, 13–15, 17, 20, 22–24, 27, 33, 41, 42, 44, 49, 56, 63, 65, 77, 79, 82, 83, 85, 90, 92–99, 101, 104–108, 110–113, 115–118, 120, 127, 132, 149, 158, 159
awareness of needs, 77, 92

canon, 81, 90
Cannon, 48, 64, 114, 134
capability goals (for peace-oriented social education), 5, 24, 26
Circles (for communication), 9, 27, 59, 60, 66, 113, 114, 134
citizenship, 4, 6, 15, 25, 79, 92, 93, 95–97, 99–101, 103–111, 113–117, 127, 129, 132, 133, 136, 147, 157, 158

citizenship education, 36, 50, 93, 108, 113, 115, 118, 119, 132, 133, 145, 148, 153, 156, 157, 159
civic engagement, 115
civil disobedience, 27
coexistence, 2, 15, 36, 78, 82, 150
cognitive realm of responsive education, 65
communication, 9, 19, 22, 23, 27, 32, 34, 35, 38, 41, 42, 44, 54, 55–59, 67, 68, 71, 76, 80–82, 84, 89, 99, 100, 101, 105, 114, 115, 121, 122, 125, 128, 135, 143, 152, 154
  inner, 21, 85, 95, 96
  outer, 96
compassionate communication, 23, 34, 55, 56, 67, 96, 101
comprehensive
  citizenship, 4, 93, 109, 117
  lessons, 110
  peace education, 154
  social education, 83
  visions of peace, 21
concept-based learning, 76, 148
conflict management, 2, 3, 8, 29, 37, 39, 65, 67, 73, 127, 152, 153, 160
conflict resolution, 12, 17, 23, 42, 45, 73, 102, 113, 121, 124, 127, 135, 145, 147, 151, 152, 153, 157, 158
constructivism, 29, 33, 63

Subject Index

contemplation, 11, 25, 61, 76, 79, 84
contextual awareness, 41, 120
cooperative learning, 12
critical literacy, 70, 156
critical pedagogy, 27
critical thinking, 52, 53, 82, 127, 153, 159
cultural capital, 57, 59, 70, 138
cultural expectations, 57
cultural universals, 80, 130
culturally-responsive educators, 39
Curriculum Adaptations, 50
curriculum integration, 74, 78, 130, 133, 135, 142, 148
curriculum hidden, 57, 58, 60, 70, 146, 150, 155
curriculum transformation, 75

developmental responsiveness, 62
Digital Media, 23
displacement, 94
domains of conflict transformation, 5, 21, 25
domains of learning, 47, 48
dominant culture, 31, 46, 49, 81, 90

e Munthu (see also 'humanness'), 8, 28
ecological imagination, 64, 132
ecological movement, 10
economic citizenship, 110
empowerment, 22, 65, 134, 146
enmity, 8, 53, 68, 78, 84, 90
environmental citizenship, 105, 106, 108
envisioning , 2, 3, 6, 7, 17, 7, 18, 21, 24, 64, 106, 133
  Peace, 5, 102
experiential education, 13

formal (explicit) curriculum, 16, 48–51, 53, 58, 59, 62–64, 70
formal instruction, 48, 61, 62, 65, 70, 82
futurism, 18, 26, 84, 85, 157

Galactic community, 46
Gayanashagowa, 150
gender balance, 31, 58, 88
gender representation, 10

geographic citizenship, 109
global synergies, 14
government standards, 37, 110

herstory, 18, 75, 115
hidden curriculum, 57, 58, 60, 70, 146, 150, 155
  transformation of, 57, 58
historical utopia, 64
holistic, 12, 62, 64, 70, 78, 160
  development, 74
  education, 65, 149
  instruction, 64, 106
  learning, 64, 79, 84, 88
humanness (see also *e Munthu*), 8, 28
humility, 8

identity, 2, 3, 35, 42, 67, 68, 86, 93, 96, 97, 99, 101, 108, 109, 116, 119, 122, 132, 139, 148, 157
illustrations, 16, 19, 44, 54, 98
imagination, 12, 19, 58, 64, 69, 77, 102, 112, 132, 138, 142, 145, 146, 150, 151
imagination intellect, 17
inclusion, 3, 16, 18, 26, 32, 38, 47, 52, 59, 62, 70, 73, 74, 85, 122, 129
inclusive visioning, 18
informal (implicit) curriculum, 56, 57, 60, 67, 115
informal instruction, 43, 60, 67, 113, 115
instrumentalism, 47, 50, 51, 70, 139, 148
integrated development, 74
intercultural cooperation, 12
interdependence, 2, 8, 21, 67, 88, 97, 109, 158
  biological, 93
  of humans, 77
  positive, 57
  spiritual, 40
international communication, 39
international policy organizations, 35
interpersonal, 20–22, 25, 56, 85, 88, 90, 97, 105, 122, 127
  domain, 20
  conflict, 38, 96
  relations, 24, 54

intrapersonal, 21, 25, 57, 85, 90, 94, 105, 122, 127
  conflict, 20, 22, 71, 85
  domain 20
  processes, 24, 88
Iroquois, 8, 26
  Constitution, 150
learning accommodations, 63
lesson plan, 24, 34, 41, 42, 67, 68, 88, 116, 117
literature
  about peacemaking, 9, 44, 85

military parents, 32
mindfulness, 94, 95, 96, 99, 101, 105, 106, 108–110, 113, 115–118, 133, 144, 149
moral development, 12, 146
multidisciplinary work, 72, 73

needs-assessment survey, 58
nongovernmental organizations, 14
nonviolent communication, 55, 135, 154

partnership, 63, 66, 67, 70, 81, 100, 101, 122, 139
peace, 1
  construal of, 3, 24
  dramatic performances of, 23, 148
  idea of, 16
  indigenous concepts of, 8
  integration of, 24, 77, 139
  liberal notions of, 63
  postmodern notions of, 63
  pursuit of, 4, 9, 15, 25, 85, 109, 113
  studies, 38, 72, 73, 75, 77, 88, 161
  visions of, 10, 18, 24, 28, 29, 43, 70, 102–104, 123
peace building, 38, 132
peace development, 6, 12, 15, 19, 22, 37, 43, 46, 54, 65, 88, 90, 99, 115, 123, 126
peace education, 2, 20
  endorsements of, 35, 36
  goals of, 19, 126
  policy, 30
  standards for, 41, 44, 46, 135
Peace Linguistics, 56, 138
Peace Partners, 67, 101
peacefulness, 8
Policy, 29–35, 37, 39–41, 43–46, 108, 116, 135, 136, 139, 150, 151, 156, 157, 160
political citizenship, 4, 113, 116
power standards, 31, 136
powerful instruction, 76, 78, 82, 87
powerful learning, 4, 72, 73, 75, 77, 79, 81, 83, 85, 87, 89, 91
powerful social education, 20, 74, 82
pragmatic education, 13
praxis, 47, 53, 61, 62, 70
principles, 5, 25, 137, 150, 161
  of a culture, 7, 8, 10, 15
  principled living, 7
proactive, 28
  citizenship, 93
  communication, 41, 42
prosocial, 6, 25, 28, 37, 58, 62, 64, 65, 70, 86, 93, 94, 99, 103, 134
  education, 47, 48
  prosocial modeling, 6
purposeful planning, 62

qualitative inquiry, 73

realms of learning, 4, 65
  affective realm of learning, 65
reconciliation, 22, 23, 133, 148
reify, 70
resistance, 11, 30, 63, 69, 132, 155
responsive curriculum, 47, 49, 51, 53, 55, 57, 59, 61, 63, 65–67, 69, 71
responsive education, 65
responsive instruction, 34, 41, 60, 62
responsive social education, 67
restoration, 9, 22, 27, 59, 61, 106, 107, 114, 123
ripples (from action), 94, 95, 106
role play, 63

satyagraha, 11, 12, 28, 228
school-centered community, 63

scientific methods of inquiry, 73
social and ecological footprint, 22, 28
social citizenship, 104, 105
social education, 1, 2, 19, 20, 22, 24, 26
   constructivist social education, 33
   disciplines of, 75, 88
   domains of, 3, 47, 48
   emergent disciplines of, 75, 88
   meaningful, 72, 74, 78, 79, 81, 87, 89, 130, 133, 136, 157
   visionary social education, 83, 87, 89, 97
social-emotional awareness, 82
social-emotional development and learning, 84, 90
social perspectives, 66
social reconstruction (ism), 13
social studies, 2, 18, 31, 32, 37, 38, 49, 50, 70, 72–74, 76, 79–83, 89, 93, 130, 131, 133, 134, 136–139, 141–143, 146–153, 155, 157–160
spirituality integration, 79
surface culture, 7, 28
sustainability, 40, 45, 46, 75, 109, 110, 138, 139
sustainability education, 45, 159
standards of complexity, 32, 33, 46
stewardship, 6, 19, 22 92, 99, 105, 117, 118
   biological, 121, 123, 126
   planetary, 21
   social, 21, 22
student activism, 63
study circles, 59
synergy, 73, 158
systemic/structural, 21, 97, 114, 122, 126, 127
   domain, 20
   challenges, 24

conflict, 20, 22, 25, 27, 28, 51, 54, 60, 63, 64, 67, 71, 85, 94, 97, 101, 104, 108, 114, 116, 119

teacher preparation, 38
the way (*Tao*), 10, 28, 151
theory of cognitive development, 33
theory of instrumentalism, 47, 50, 51
thinking aloud, 60, 71
transdisciplinarity, 73, 87, 90, 146, 150–152, 154, 156
transdisciplinary, 150, 151
   curriculum, 73, 90
   learning, 4, 72, 73, 75–77, 79, 81, 83, 85–87, 89, 91
transformation-oriented pedagogy, 74
transformation of knowledge, 61
transformative curriculum, 75

unity, 7, 8, 12, 31, 37, 78, 88, 106, 137
unity-based worldview, 14, 78

values-clarification activities, 82
violence, 2, 6, 8, 12–15, 18–24, 27, 28, 31, 36, 42, 43, 45, 51, 52, 56, 63, 64, 67, 78, 79, 97, 98, 101, 103, 107, 108, 113, 117, 121, 122, 124–127, 133, 136, 140, 148
visionary artwork, 103
visionary learning, 19, 25, 26, 45, 69, 89
visionary lessons, 61, 89
visioning (as curriculum), 18
vocabulary curriculum, 55

Wolokokiciapi, 8
Wowahwala, 8

yin and yang, 10

GPSR Compliance
The European Union's (EU) General Product Safety Regulation (GPSR) is a set of rules that requires consumer products to be safe and our obligations to ensure this.

If you have any concerns about our products, you can contact us on

ProductSafety@springernature.com

In case Publisher is established outside the EU, the EU authorized representative is:

Springer Nature Customer Service Center GmbH
Europaplatz 3
69115 Heidelberg, Germany

www.ingramcontent.com/pod-product-compliance
Lightning Source LLC
LaVergne TN
LVHW041955060526
838200LV00002B/25